The Military Propeller Aircraft Guide

The Military Propeller Aircraft Guide

Editor: David Donald

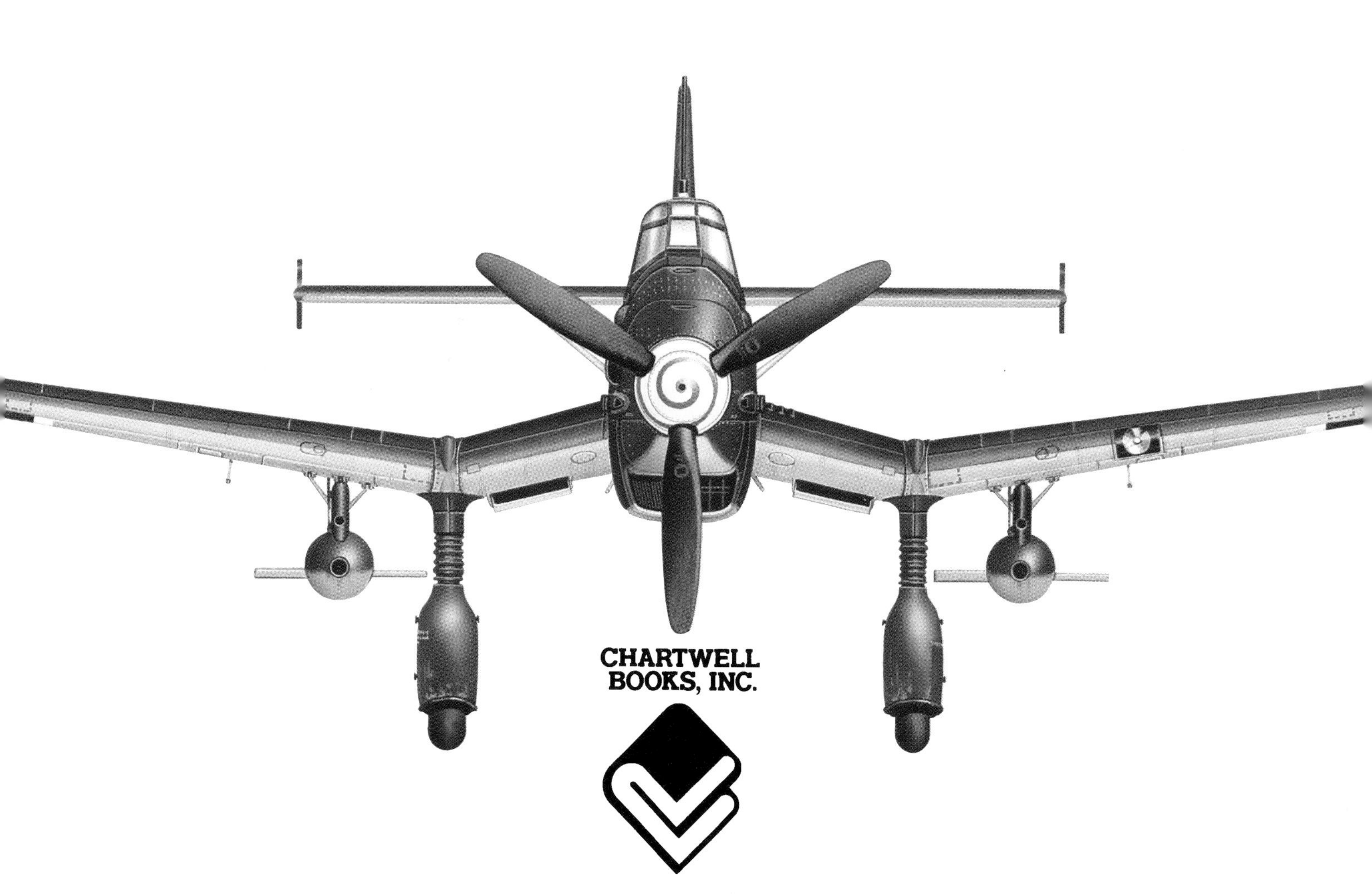

CHARTWELL
BOOKS, INC.

Published by
CHARTWELL BOOKS, INC.
A Division of **BOOK SALES, INC.**
114 Northfield Avenue
Edison, New Jersey 08837

Some of this material has previously appeared in the
Orbis reference set 'Airplane'.

ISBN: 0-7858-1023-4

Editorial and design by
Brown Packaging Books Ltd
Bradley's Close
74–77 White Lion Street
London N1 9PF

Editor: David Donald

Printed in The Czech Republic

Contents

Fokker Dr.I

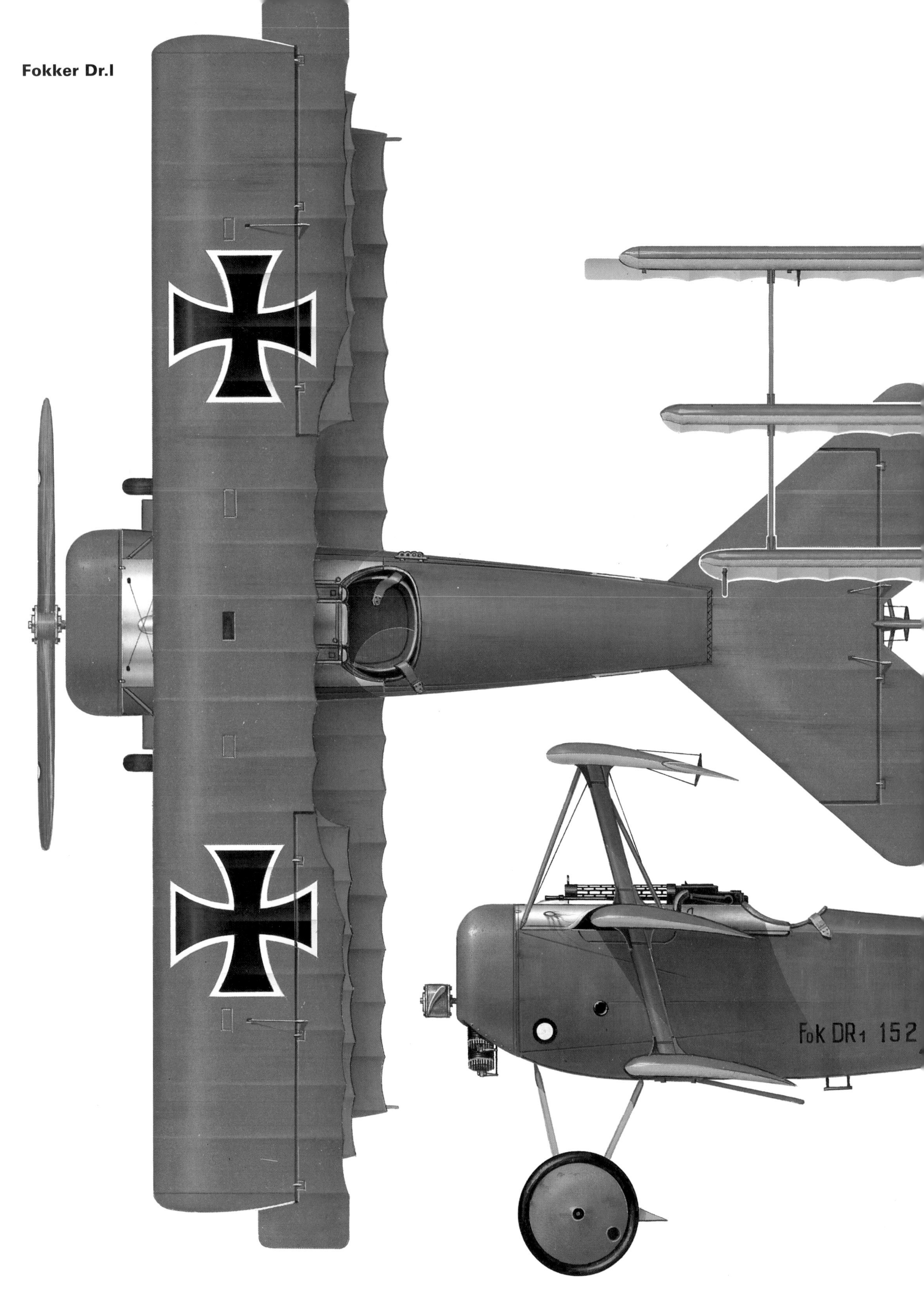

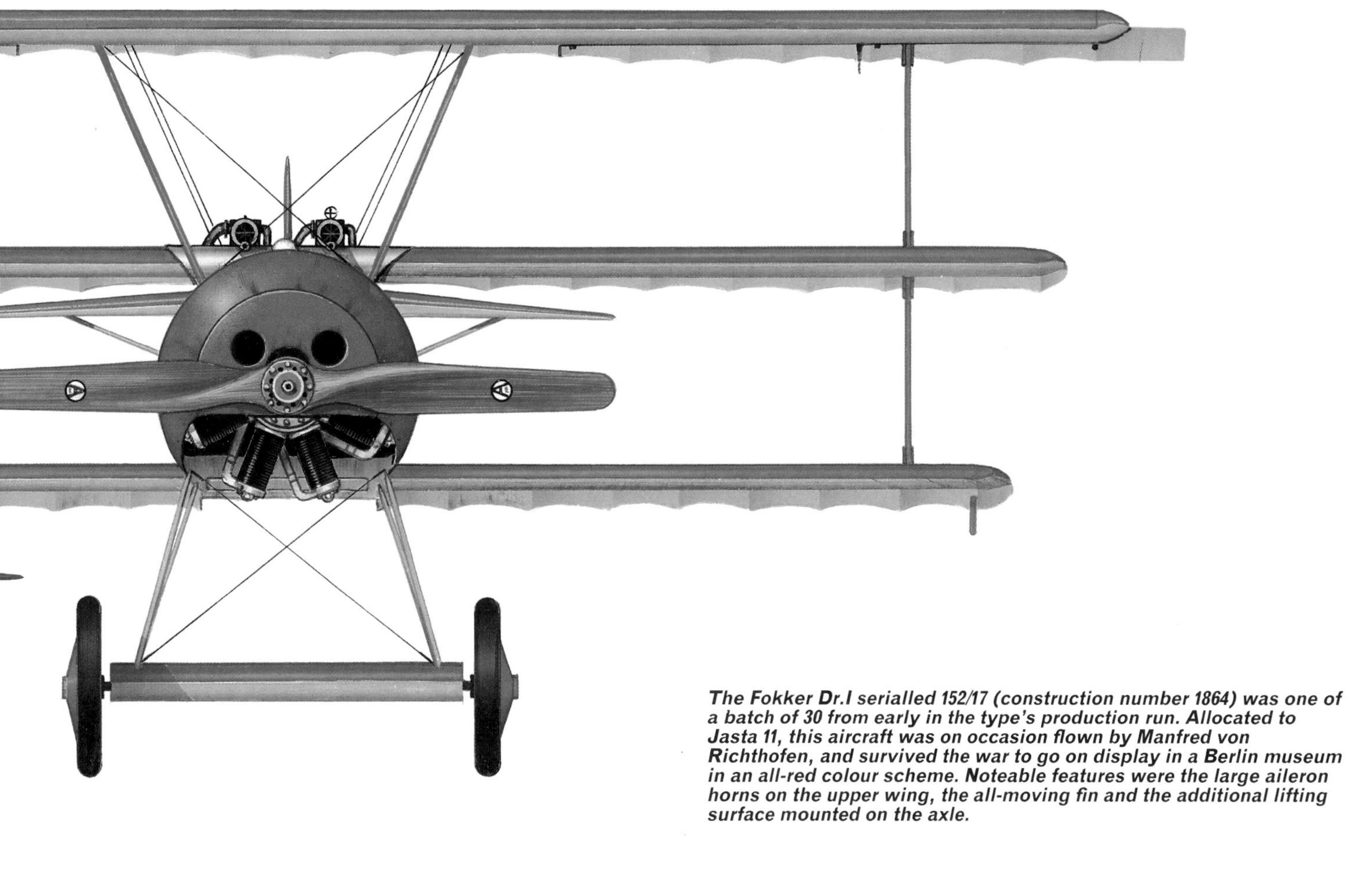

The Fokker Dr.I serialled 152/17 (construction number 1864) was one of a batch of 30 from early in the type's production run. Allocated to Jasta 11, this aircraft was on occasion flown by Manfred von Richthofen, and survived the war to go on display in a Berlin museum in an all-red colour scheme. Noteable features were the large aileron horns on the upper wing, the all-moving fin and the additional lifting surface mounted on the axle.

Specification

Fokker Dr.I

Type: single-seat fighting scout

Powerplant: one 82-kW (110-hp) Oberursel Ur.II nine-cylinder rotary piston engine

Performance: maximum speed 185 km/h (115 mph) at sea level; 165 km/h (103 mph) at 4000 m (13,125 ft); climb to 1000 m (3,280 ft) 2 minutes 55 seconds; service ceiling 6100 m (20,015 ft); range 300 km (186 miles); endurance 1 hour 20 minutes

Weights: empty 406 kg (894 lb); maximum take-off 586 kg (1,291 lb)

Dimensions: span upper 7.12 m (23 ft 7 in), centre 6.23 m (20 ft 5¼ in), lower 5.7 m (18 ft 8½ in); length 5.77 m (18 ft 11 in); height 2.95 m (9 ft 8 in); wing area, including axle fairing 18.66 m^2 (200.85 sq ft)

Armament: two 7.92 mm (0.31 in) LMG 08/15 machine-guns, each with 500 rounds

*Few aircraft were more colourful than the **Albatros D.Vs**, and this example is no exception. Later aircraft were delivered with pre-dyed 'lozenge' fabric on the wing fabric. Jasta 5 was the best-known of the Albatros operators, its ranks including many important aces. This particular aircraft was a **D.V**, and is believed to have been flown by Klein. If so, this is the aircraft in which he was shot down by McCudden.*

Specification
Albatros D.V
Type: single-seat scout fighter
Powerplant: one 134/149-kW (180/200-hp) Mercedes D.IIIa inline piston engine
Dimensions: wing span (upper) 9.00 m (29 ft 6 in); wing span (lower) 8.73 m (28 ft 8 in); length 7.36 m (24 ft 2 in); height 2.75 m (9 ft 0 in); wing area 20.86 m^2 (224.5 sq ft)
Weights: empty 680 kg (1,500 lb); maximum loaded 915 kg (2,017 lb)
Performance: maximum speed 170 km/h (105 mph); time to 1000 m (3,280 ft) 4.4 minutes; time to 3000 m (9,842 ft) 14.5 minutes; time to 5000 m (16,404 ft) 35 minutes; service ceiling 5700 m (18,700 ft); endurance 2 hours
Armament: two fixed forward-firing 7.92-mm (0.31-in) LMG 08/51 machine-guns firing through propeller arc

A Camel of 'B' Flight, No. 210 Sqn, RAF, on the Western Front. After the old No. 10 (Naval) Sqn, RNAS, was re-numbered No. 210 in the Royal Air Force on 1 April 1918 the horizontal bars (black for 'A' Flight, red for 'B' and blue for 'C', all separated by white bars) were omitted from the nose, and the flight was simply denoted by a letter just aft of the cockpit. The squadron was heavily involved in fighting at the time of the German offensive in mid-1918, before returning to routine coastal patrol work in July.

Specification

Sopwith F.1 Camel (Clerget)
Type: single-seat fighting scout
Powerplant: one 97-kW (130-hp) Clerget 9-cylinder air-cooled rotary piston engine
Performance: maximum speed 188 km/h (117 mph) at sea level; climb to 3050 m (10,000 ft) in 10 minutes 35 seconds; service ceiling 5790 m (19,000 ft); endurance 2 hours 30 minutes
Weights: empty 421 kg (929 lb); maximum take-off 659 kg (1,453 lb)
Dimensions: span 8.53 m (28 ft 0 in); length 5.72 m (18 ft 9 in); height 2.6 m (8 ft 6 in); wing area 21.46 m^2 (231 sq ft)
Armament: two 7.7-mm (0.303-in) Vickers machine-guns on nose and synchronised to fire through the propeller, plus four 11.35-kg (25-lb) bombs carried on external racks below the fuselage

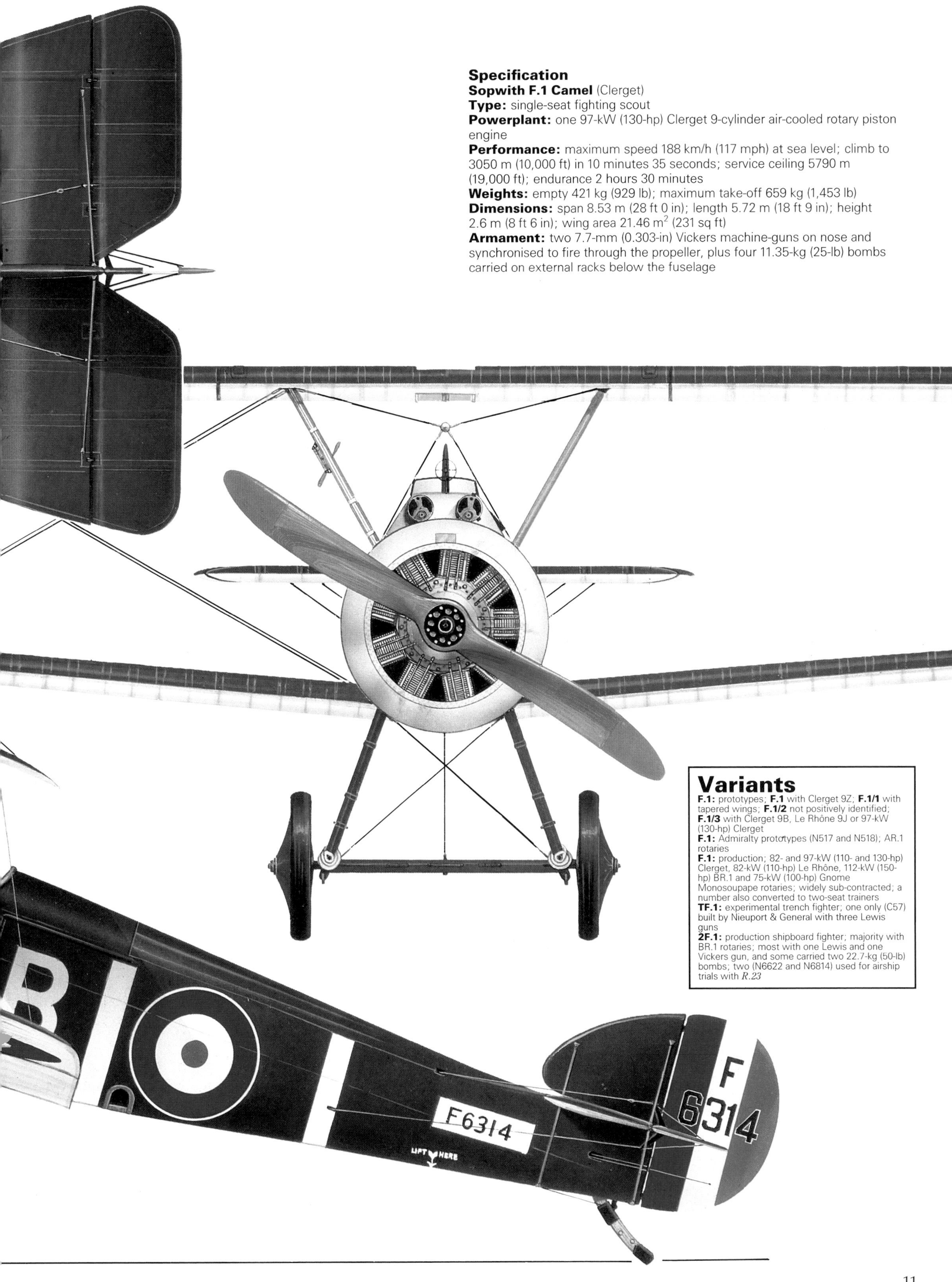

Variants

F.1: prototypes; **F.1** with Clerget 9Z; **F.1/1** with tapered wings; **F.1/2** not positively identified; **F.1/3** with Clerget 9B, Le Rhône 9J or 97-kW (130-hp) Clerget
F.1: Admiralty prototypes (N517 and N518); AR.1 rotaries
F.1: production; 82- and 97-kW (110- and 130-hp) Clerget, 82-kW (110-hp) Le Rhône, 112-kW (150-hp) BR.1 and 75-kW (100-hp) Gnome Monosoupape rotaries; widely sub-contracted; a number also converted to two-seat trainers
TF.1: experimental trench fighter; one only (C57) built by Nieuport & General with three Lewis guns
2F.1: production shipboard fighter; majority with BR.1 rotaries; most with one Lewis and one Vickers gun, and some carried two 22.7-kg (50-lb) bombs; two (N6622 and N6814) used for airship trials with *R.23*

Airco D.H.4 (Eagle VIII)

Without doubt the best Airco D.H.4s were those powered by the 280-kW (375-hp) Eagle VIII, but this engine was costly and in short supply (and, because of its bigger propeller, needed longer landing gears). Many other engines were therefore fitted, most of the earlier machines having the RAF.3a, a water-cooled V-12 of only 149-kW (200-hp) produced by the Royal Aircraft Factory. A7712 was one of the RAF-engined machines, built by Airco in summer 1917 and delivered to No. 18 Sqn RFC, which with No. 49 Sqn used the RAF-engined version exclusively from June 1917. The frontal radiator tapered slightly from top to bottom (the reverse of the BHP version) and had a single exhaust stack. At first the valuable D.H.4s were kept above 4572 m (15,000 ft), but during the crucial days of March 1918 No. 18 Sqn was ordered over the front at low level to harass the advancing enemy troops.

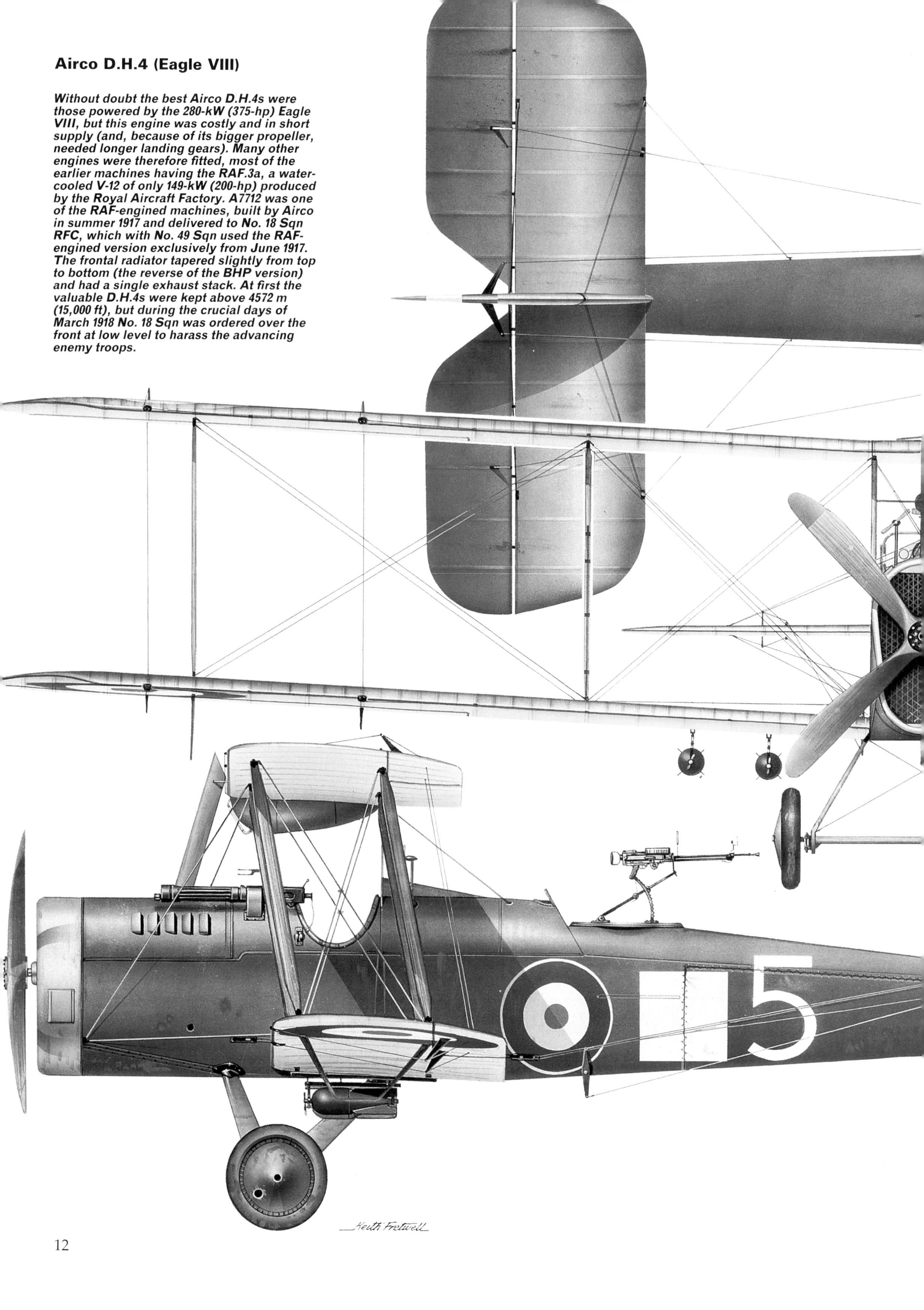

Specification
Airco D.H.4 (Eagle VIII)

Type: two-seat bomber
Powerplant: one 280-kW (375-hp) Rolls-Royce Eagle VIII water-cooled V-12 piston engine
Performance: maximum speed 230 km/h (143 mph) at sea level; cruising speed about 174 km/h (108 mph); time to reach 4572 m (15,000 ft) 16.5 minutes; service ceiling 6700 m (22,000 ft); endurance (maximum) 6 hours 45 minutes
Weights: empty 1083 kg (2,387 lb); loaded (clean) 1575 kg (3,472 lb), (two 104-kg/230-lb bombs) 1784 kg (3,932 lb)
Dimensions: span 12.92 m (42 ft 4.625 in); length (Eagle) 9.347 m (30 ft 8 in); height (Eagle VIII) 3.353 m (11 ft 0 in); wing area 40.32 m^2 (434 sq ft)
Armament: one 7.7-mm (0.303-in) Vickers machine-gun firing ahead; single or twin Lewis of same calibre mounted on observer's Scarff ring; racks under lower wing for two bombs of 104 kg (230 lb), four of 50.8 kg (112 lb), depth charges or other stores

Specification

Breguet Bre.19 A.2

Type: two-seat day bomber

Powerplant: one 383-kW (513-hp) Renault 12Kd water-cooled 12-cylinder Vee engine

Performance: maximum speed 235 km/h (146 mph) at sea level; climb to 5000 m (16,405 ft) in 29 minutes 50 seconds; absolute ceiling 6900 m (22,640 ft); maximum range 1200 km (746 miles)

Weights: empty 1722 kg (3,796 lb); normal loaded 2347 kg (5,174 lb); maximum take-off 3110 kg (6,856 lb)

Dimensions: span 14.83 m (48 ft 7¾ in); length 9.51 m (31 ft 2½ in); height 3.69 m (12 ft 1¼ in); wing area 50.00 m^2 (538.2 sq ft)

Armament: one forward-firing synchronised Vickers 7.7-mm (0.303-in) machine-gun with 500 rounds, two Lewis 7.7-mm (0.303-in) guns on Scarff TO-7 ring mounting on rear cockpit and one ventral 7.7-mm (0.303-in) gun with 1,522 rounds, plus a maximum internal bombload of 400 kg (882 lb) and 400 kg (882 lb) on external racks

Unquestionably the most illustrious Breguet 19 was the record-breaking Super-Bidon* Point d'Interrogation (Question Mark)*, whose manufacture was sponsored by François Coty, the perfume magnate. After Dieudonné Costes and Maurice Bellonte had failed to fly the Atlantic in July 1929, a direct-drive Hispano-Suiza 12Lb engine was fitted and in this form the aircraft established a new world record of 7906 km (4,913 miles) when the same crew flew from Le Bourget to Tsitsihkar in Manchuria on 27-29 September 1929. It was again re-engined, this time with a 485-kW (650-hp) Hispano-Suiza 12Nb engine, and made the first direct aeroplane flight from Paris to New York. Thereafter it embarked on a 'Voyage of Friendship' in the USA, its landing points being recorded on the rear fuselage chevron as shown in this illustration. Other remarkable achievements are also recorded between the chevrons.

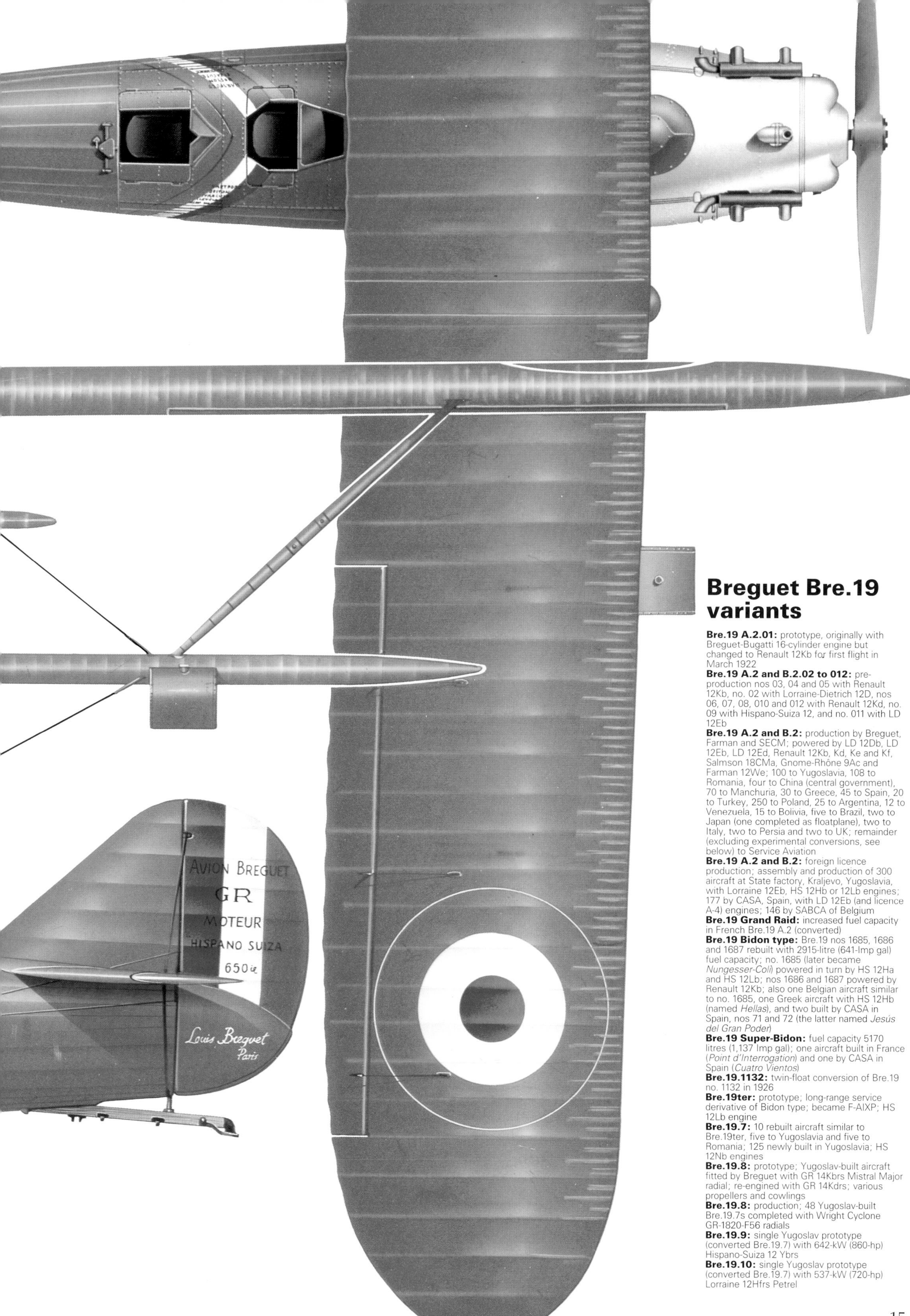

Breguet Bre.19 variants

Bre.19 A.2.01: prototype, originally with Breguet-Bugatti 16-cylinder engine but changed to Renault 12Kb for first flight in March 1922
Bre.19 A.2 and B.2.02 to 012: pre-production nos 03, 04 and 05 with Renault 12Kb, no. 02 with Lorraine-Dietrich 12D, nos 06, 07, 08, 010 and 012 with Renault 12Kd, no. 09 with Hispano-Suiza 12, and no. 011 with LD 12Eb
Bre.19 A.2 and B.2: production by Breguet, Farman and SECM; powered by LD 12Db, LD 12Eb, LD 12Ed, Renault 12Kb, Kd, Ke and Kf, Salmson 18CMa, Gnome-Rhône 9Ac and Farman 12We; 100 to Yugoslavia, 108 to Romania, four to China (central government), 70 to Manchuria, 30 to Greece, 45 to Spain, 20 to Turkey, 250 to Poland, 25 to Argentina, 12 to Venezuela, 15 to Bolivia, five to Brazil, two to Japan (one completed as floatplane), two to Italy, two to Persia and two to UK; remainder (excluding experimental conversions, see below) to Service Aviation
Bre.19 A.2 and B.2: foreign licence production; assembly and production of 300 aircraft at State factory, Kraljevo, Yugoslavia, with Lorraine 12Eb, HS 12Hb or 12Lb engines; 177 by CASA, Spain, with LD 12Eb (and licence A-4) engines; 146 by SABCA of Belgium
Bre.19 Grand Raid: increased fuel capacity in French Bre.19 A.2 (converted)
Bre.19 Bidon type: Bre.19 nos 1685, 1686 and 1687 rebuilt with 2915-litre (641-Imp gal) fuel capacity; no. 1685 (later became *Nungesser-Coli*) powered in turn by HS 12Ha and HS 12Lb; nos 1686 and 1687 powered by Renault 12Kb; also one Belgian aircraft similar to no. 1685, one Greek aircraft with HS 12Hb (named *Hellas*), and two built by CASA in Spain, nos 71 and 72 (the latter named *Jesús del Gran Poder*)
Bre.19 Super-Bidon: fuel capacity 5170 litres (1,137 Imp gal); one aircraft built in France (*Point d'Interrogation*) and one by CASA in Spain (*Cuatro Vientos*)
Bre.19.1132: twin-float conversion of Bre.19 no. 1132 in 1926
Bre.19ter: prototype; long-range service derivative of Bidon type; became F-AIXP; HS 12Lb engine
Bre.19.7: 10 rebuilt aircraft similar to Bre.19ter, five to Yugoslavia and five to Romania; 125 newly built in Yugoslavia; HS 12Nb engines
Bre.19.8: prototype; Yugoslav-built aircraft fitted by Breguet with GR 14Kbrs Mistral Major radial; re-engined with GR 14Kdrs; various propellers and cowlings
Bre.19.8: production; 48 Yugoslav-built Bre.19.7s completed with Wright Cyclone GR-1820-F56 radials
Bre.19.9: single Yugoslav prototype (converted Bre.19.7) with 642-kW (860-hp) Hispano-Suiza 12 Ybrs
Bre.19.10: single Yugoslav prototype (converted Bre.19.7) with 537-kW (720-hp) Lorraine 12Hfrs Petrel

Bulldog Mk IIA

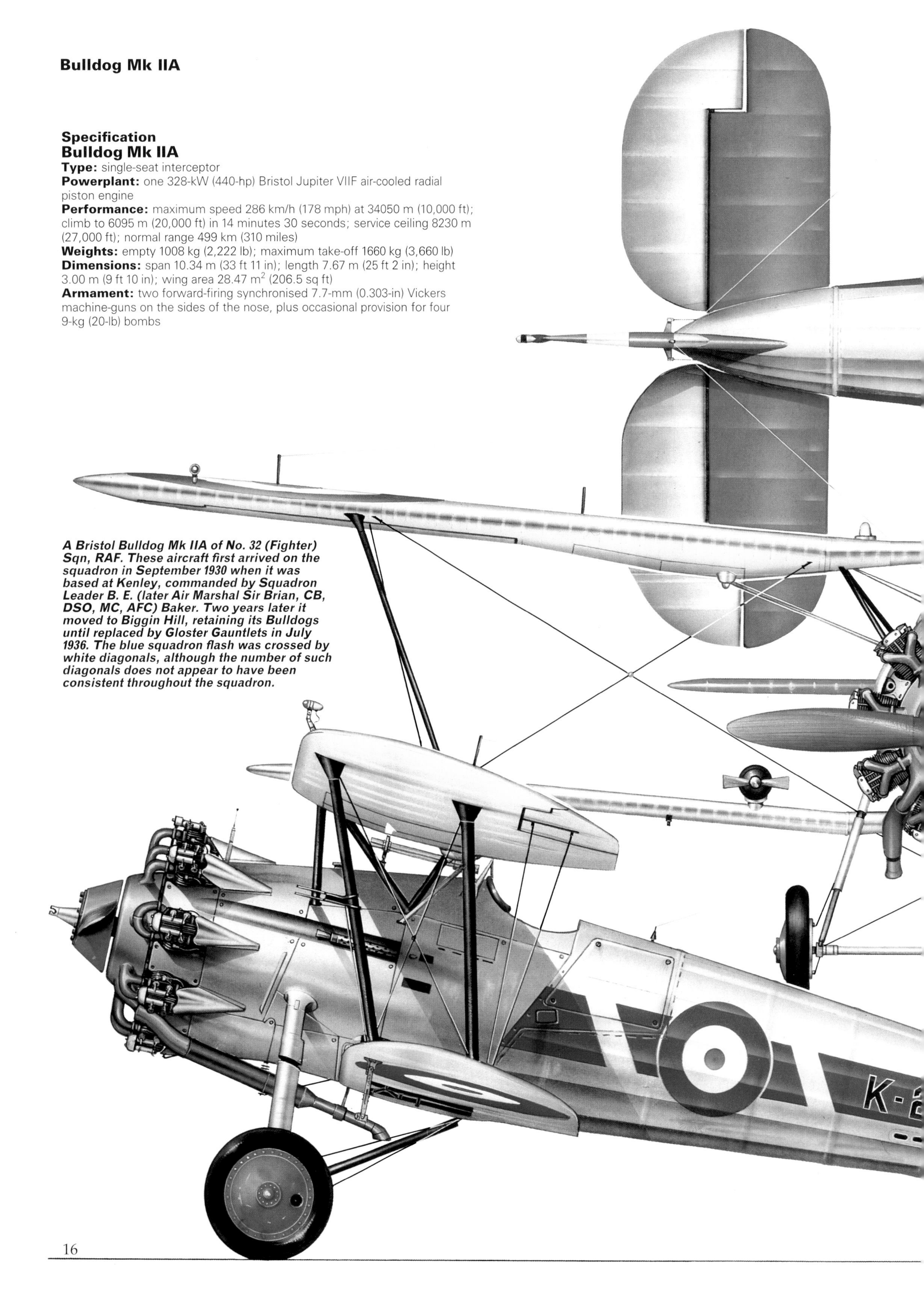

Specification
Bulldog Mk IIA

Type: single-seat interceptor
Powerplant: one 328-kW (440-hp) Bristol Jupiter VIIF air-cooled radial piston engine
Performance: maximum speed 286 km/h (178 mph) at 34050 m (10,000 ft); climb to 6095 m (20,000 ft) in 14 minutes 30 seconds; service ceiling 8230 m (27,000 ft); normal range 499 km (310 miles)
Weights: empty 1008 kg (2,222 lb); maximum take-off 1660 kg (3,660 lb)
Dimensions: span 10.34 m (33 ft 11 in); length 7.67 m (25 ft 2 in); height 3.00 m (9 ft 10 in); wing area 28.47 m^2 (206.5 sq ft)
Armament: two forward-firing synchronised 7.7-mm (0.303-in) Vickers machine-guns on the sides of the nose, plus occasional provision for four 9-kg (20-lb) bombs

A Bristol Bulldog Mk IIA of No. 32 (Fighter) Sqn, RAF. These aircraft first arrived on the squadron in September 1930 when it was based at Kenley, commanded by Squadron Leader B. E. (later Air Marshal Sir Brian, CB, DSO, MC, AFC) Baker. Two years later it moved to Biggin Hill, retaining its Bulldogs until replaced by Gloster Gauntlets in July 1936. The blue squadron flash was crossed by white diagonals, although the number of such diagonals does not appear to have been consistent throughout the squadron.

K
2481
Keith Fretwell.

Gloster Gladiator Mk I

A Gladiator Mk I of the second production batch shown in the markings of No. 73 (Fighter) Sqn. When deliveries of this fighter were first made in June that year the squadron was commanded by Squadron Leader Eric Stanley Finch at Debden, but moved to Digby in November where it gave up the biplanes in favour of the Hurricane the following July. As was fairly common in Fighter Command at the time, the yellow wheel discs and propeller boss denoted a 'B' Flight aircraft.

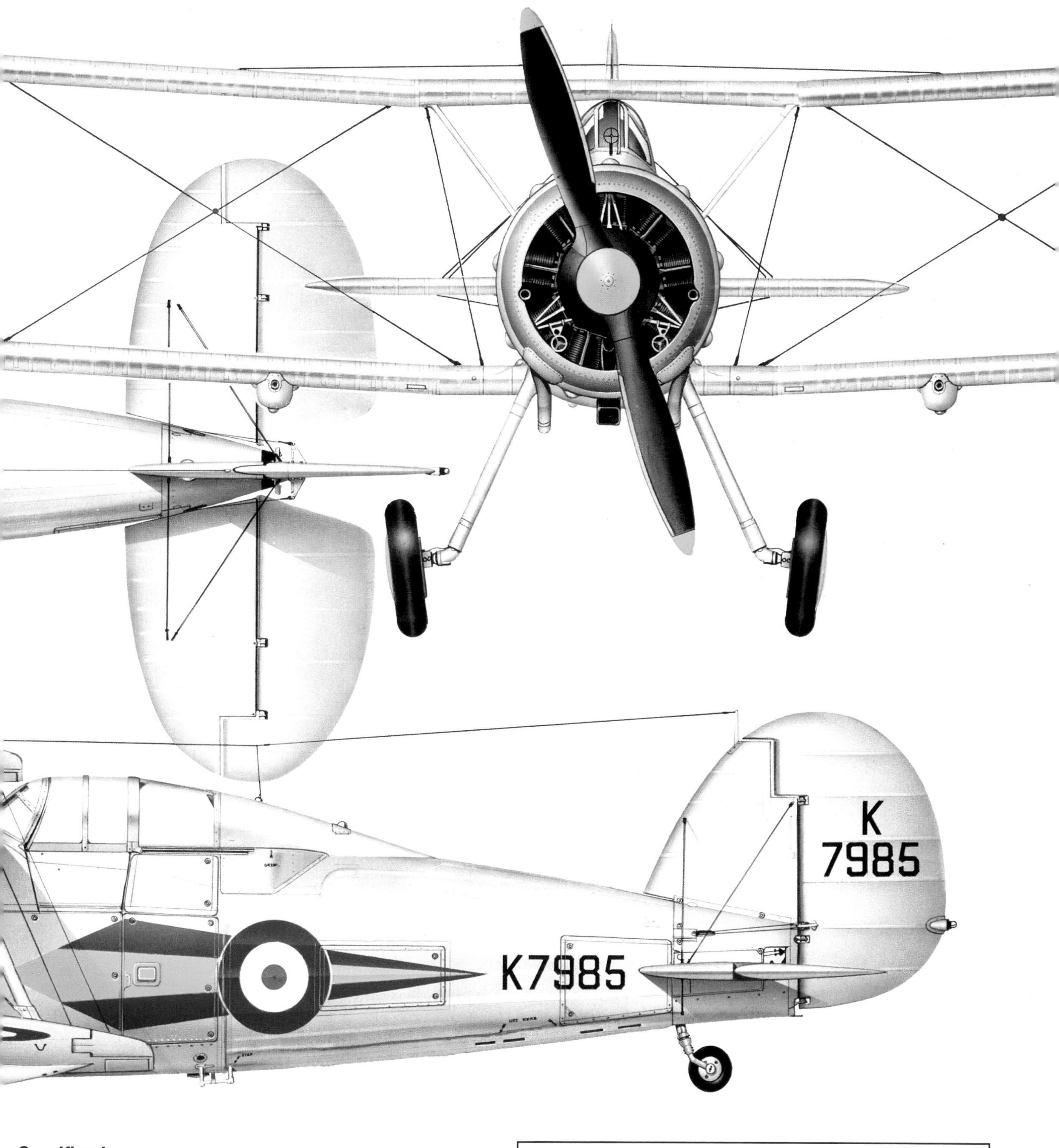

Specification
Gloster Gladiator Mk I

Type: single-seat interceptor biplane

Powerplant: one 627-kW (840-hp) Bristol Mercury IX air-cooled radial piston engine

Performance: maximum speed 407 km/h (253 mph) at 4420 m (14,500 ft); climb to 6095 m (20,000 ft) in 9 minutes 30 seconds; service ceiling 10060 m (33,000 ft); range 547 km (340 miles)

Weights: empty 1565 kg (3,450 lb); maximum take-off 2155 kg (4,750 lb)

Dimensions: span 9.83 m (32 ft 3 in); length 8.36 m (27 ft 5 in); height 3.15 m (10 ft 4 in); wing area 30.01 m^2 (323.0 sq ft)

Armament: two nose-mounted Vickers Mk V 7.7-mm (0.303-in) machine-guns each with 600 rounds, and two wing-mounted 7.7-mm (0.303-in) Lewis machine-guns each with one 97-round drum; later aircraft had all guns changed to Brownings, each fuselage gun with 600 rounds and each wing gun with 400 rounds

Gloster Gladiator variants

SS.37: one prototype (K5200) to Specification F7/30; first flown September 1934

Gladiator Mk I: 23 aircraft (K6129-K6151) completed with Vickers and Lewis guns; production for RAF in 1936-37

Gladiator Mk I: 208 aircraft (K7892-K8055, L7608-L7623 and L8005-L8032); production in 1937-38 for RAF; most completed with Browning guns, and some later converted to Mk II; some later passed to Egypt, Iraq and Greece

Gladiator Mk I: 147 aircraft built for export (Belgium 22, China 36, Eire 4, Greece 2, Latvia 26, Lithuania 14, Norway 6 and Sweden 37 (**J8**)

Gladiator Mk I: two aircraft (K6129 and K8039) converted to Sea Gladiator standard for trials

Sea Gladiator (Interim): 38 aircraft (N2265-N2302) modified on Mk II production line for Royal Navy

Gladiator Mk II: 252 aircraft (N2303-N2314, N5575-N5594, N5620-N5649, N5680-N5729, N5750-N5789, N5810-N5859 and N5875-N5924) for RAF; Mercury VIII or VIIIAS driving Fairey Reed 3-bladed propeller; 15 aircraft (N5835-N5849) sold to Portugal, and 6 (N5919-N5924) to Norway before delivery to RAF; others later passed to Finland (33), Greece (about 6), Egypt (27), South Africa (11) and Iraq (5)

Gladiator Mk II (J8A): 18 export aircraft for Sweden

Sea Gladiator: 60 full-standard aircraft for Royal Navy (N5500-N5549, N5565-N5574) with arrester hook, dinghy stowage and provision for two additional Browning guns in top wing

Hawker Hart

Specification

Hawker Hart

Type: two-seat light day bomber

Powerplant: one 392-kW (525-hp) Rolls-Royce Kestrel IB 12-cylinder Vee liquid-cooled engine

Performance: maximum speed 296 km/h (184 mph) at 1525 m (5,000 ft); climb to 3050 m (10,000 ft) in 8 minutes 20 seconds; service ceiling 6506 m (21,350 ft); range 692 km (430 miles)

Weights: empty 1148 kg (2,530 lb); maximum take-off 2066 kg (4,554 lb)

Dimensions: span 11.35 m (37 ft 3 in); length 8.94 m (29 ft 4 in); height 3.17 m (10 ft 5 in); wing area 32.33 m^2 (384.0 sq ft)

Armament: one fixed forward-firing 7.7-mm (0.303-in) Vickers Mk II or III machine-gun in port side of nose and one 7.7-mm (0.303-in) Lewis gun on rear cockpit mounting, plus a bombload of up to 236 kg (520 lb)

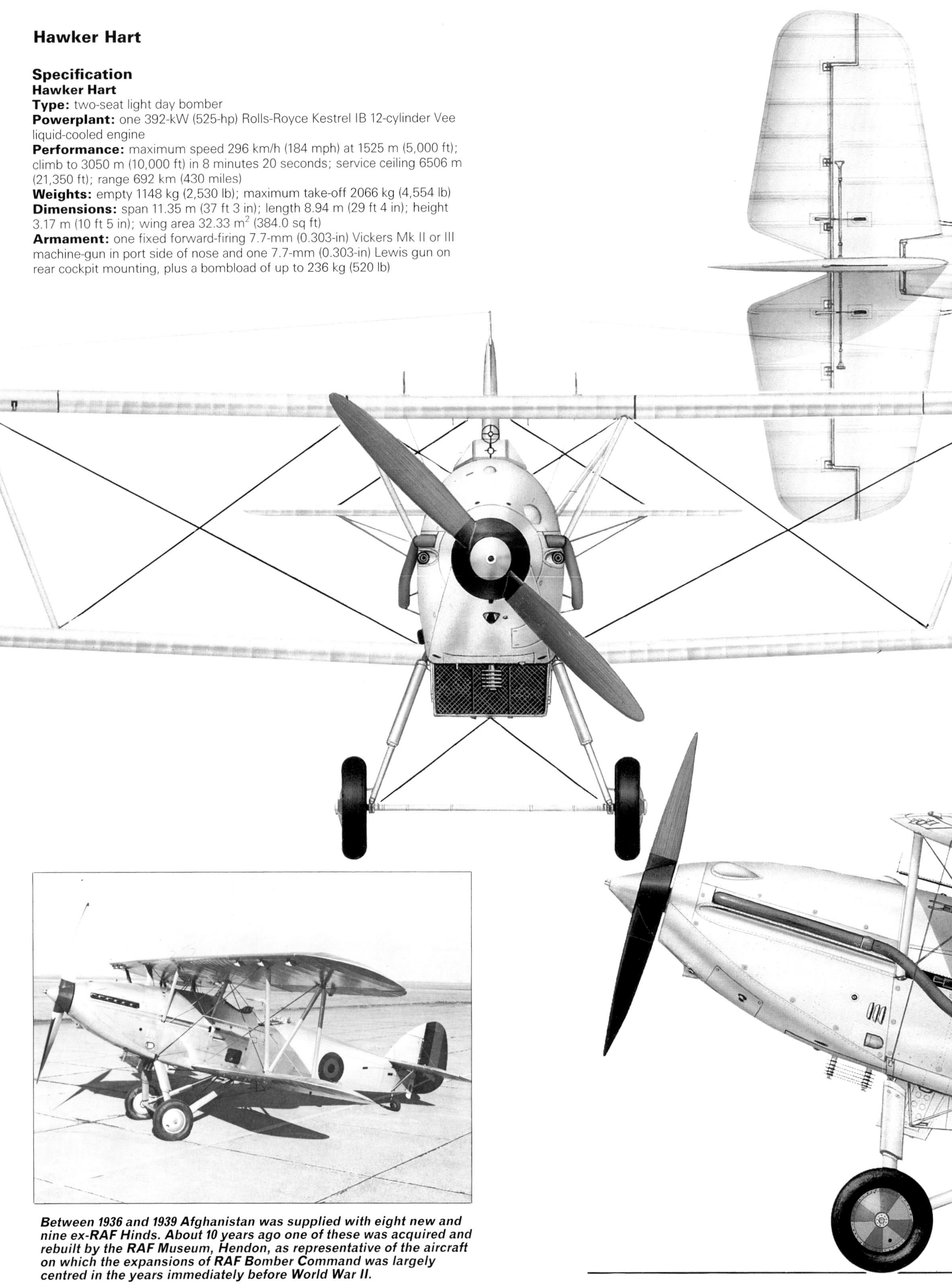

Between 1936 and 1939 Afghanistan was supplied with eight new and nine ex-RAF Hinds. About 10 years ago one of these was acquired and rebuilt by the RAF Museum, Hendon, as representative of the aircraft on which the expansions of RAF Bomber Command was largely centred in the years immediately before World War II.

Displaying the distinctive flashes of No. 604 (County of Middlesex) Sqn, Auxiliary Air Force, this Hawker Demon also bears the county badge (three seaxes) on the fin, and the commanding officer's pennant below the front cockpit sill. Based at Hendon from the date of its formation in 1930 until the outbreak of war in September 1939, No. 604 Sqn started life as a light bomber auxiliary squadron but changed to Demon fighters in 1935, retaining them until becoming a night fighter squadron with Blenheims. Among the squadron's famous pilots who flew Demons was Flight Lieutenant (later Group Captain) John Cunningham.

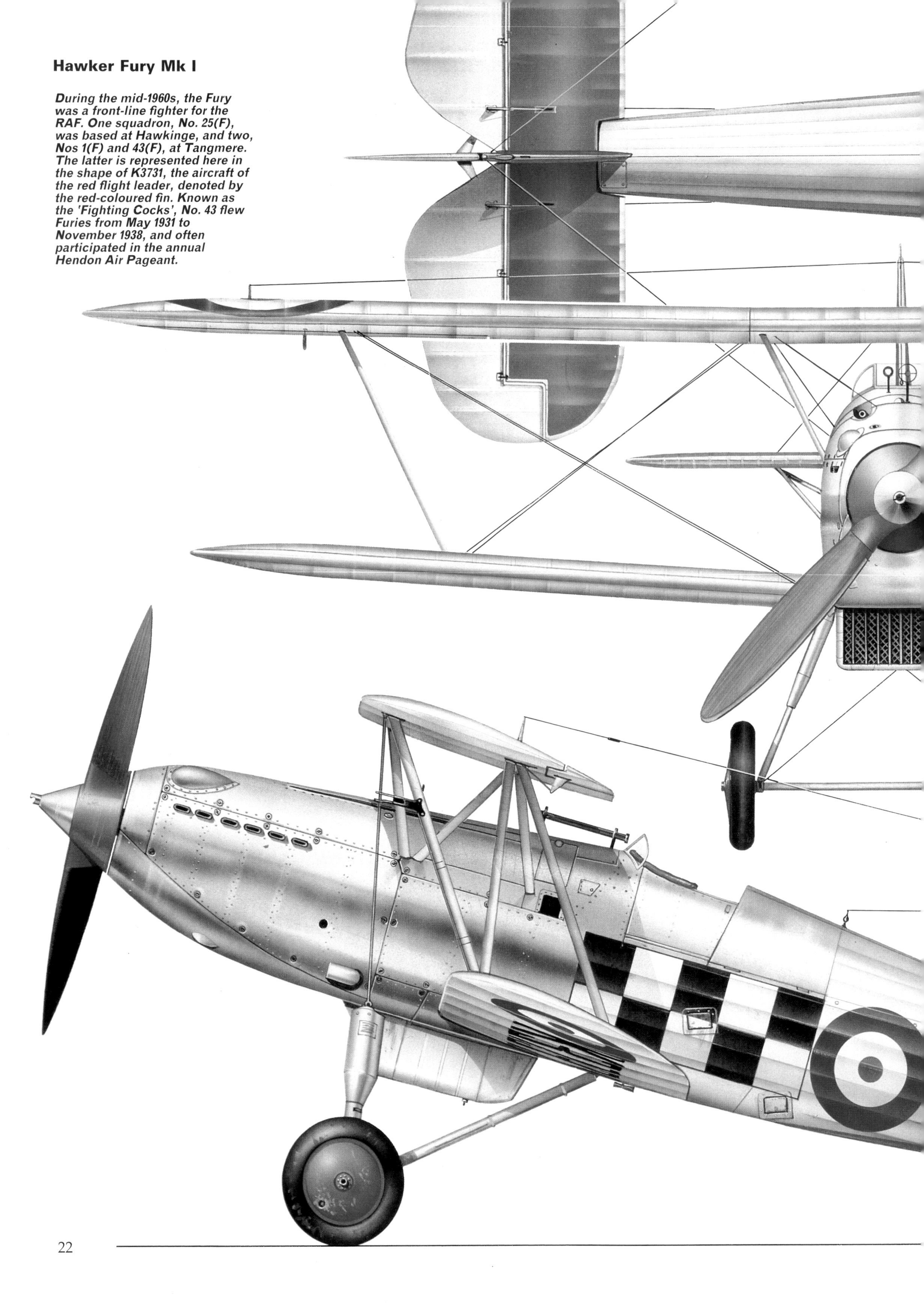

Hawker Fury Mk I

During the mid-1960s, the Fury was a front-line fighter for the RAF. One squadron, No. 25(F), was based at Hawkinge, and two, Nos 1(F) and 43(F), at Tangmere. The latter is represented here in the shape of K3731, the aircraft of the red flight leader, denoted by the red-coloured fin. Known as the 'Fighting Cocks', No. 43 flew Furies from May 1931 to November 1938, and often participated in the annual Hendon Air Pageant.

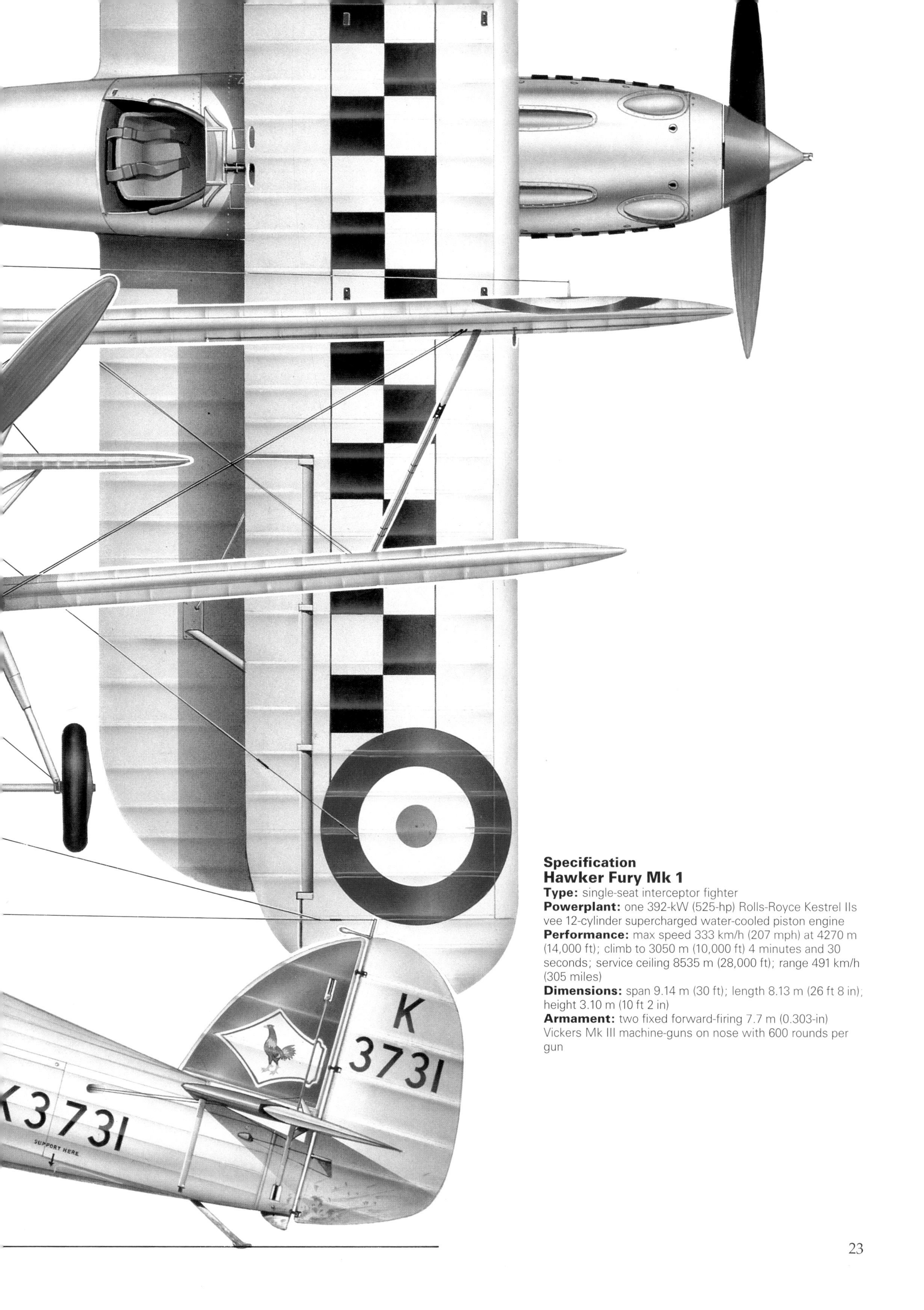

Specification
Hawker Fury Mk 1
Type: single-seat interceptor fighter
Powerplant: one 392-kW (525-hp) Rolls-Royce Kestrel IIs vee 12-cylinder supercharged water-cooled piston engine
Performance: max speed 333 km/h (207 mph) at 4270 m (14,000 ft); climb to 3050 m (10,000 ft) 4 minutes and 30 seconds; service ceiling 8535 m (28,000 ft); range 491 km/h (305 miles)
Dimensions: span 9.14 m (30 ft); length 8.13 m (26 ft 8 in); height 3.10 m (10 ft 2 in)
Armament: two fixed forward-firing 7.7 m (0.303-in) Vickers Mk III machine-guns on nose with 600 rounds per gun

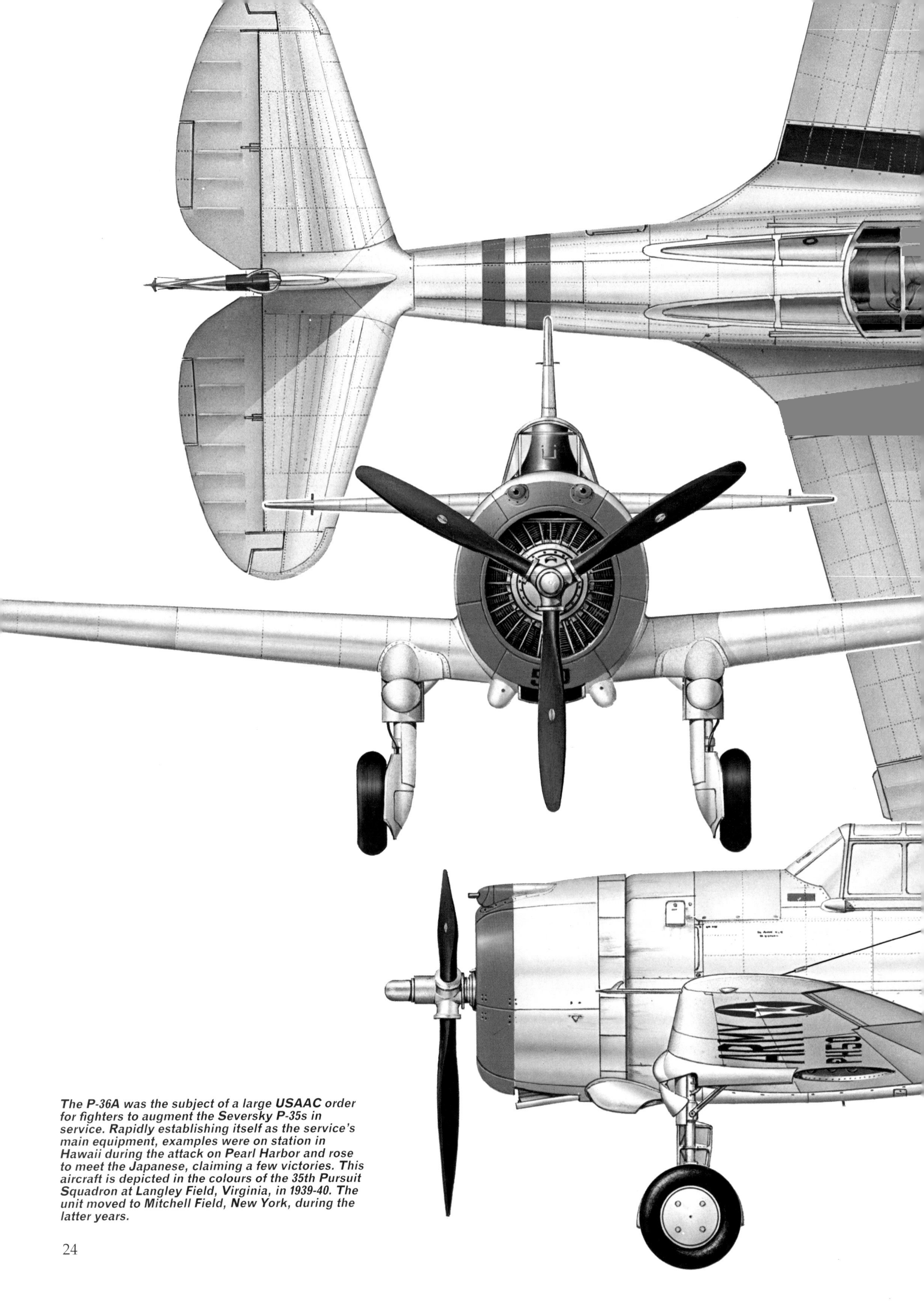

The ***P-36A*** *was the subject of a large* ***USAAC*** *order for fighters to augment the* ***Seversky P-35s*** *in service.* ***R****apidly establishing itself as the service's main equipment, examples were on station in* ***H****awaii during the attack on* ***P****earl* ***H****arbor and rose to meet the* ***J****apanese, claiming a few victories.* ***T****his aircraft is depicted in the colours of the 35th* ***P****ursuit* ***S****quadron at* ***L****angley* ***F****ield,* ***V****irginia, in 1939-40.* ***T****he unit moved to* ***M****itchell* ***F****ield,* ***N****ew* ***Y****ork, during the latter years.*

Specification
Curtiss P-36A Hawk

Type: single-seat pursuit fighter and advanced trainer
Powerplant: one 783-kW Wright R-1830-13 piston engine
Performance: max speed 480 km/h at 3000 m; cruising speed 430 km/h; service ceiling 10000 m; range 1300 km
Weights: empty weight 2070 kg; gross weight 2700 kg
Dimensions: wing span 11.4 m; length 8.7 m; height 3.7 m
Armament: two 0.030-in machine-guns

Trainer variants

NA-16: original prototype, 298-kW (400-hp) R-975 engine; modified as NA-18 with enclosed cockpit and 448-kW (600-hp) R-1340
NA-19: USAAC BT-9 with R-975, fixed slats, 42 built
NA-19A: USAAC BT-9A with nose and dorsal 7.62-mm (0.3-in) guns and recording camera, 40 for USAAC Reserve
NA-22: ninth BT-9 temporarily evaluated as primary trainer, open cockpits, Townend-ring cowl, simpler equipment
NA-23: USAAC BT-9B for 1937 production, 117 built
NA-28: US Navy model, NJ-1, 373-kW (500-hp) R-1340-6, 40 built (last flown temporarily as NJ-2 with 366-kW/490-hp XV-770-4)
NA-29: USAAC Reserve BT-9C with nose and dorsal guns, 67 built; first completed as Y1BT-10 with 448-kW (600-hp) R-1340 and another with RC-1A-type wings and tail as BT-9D

NA-30: Y1BT-10 (see above)
NA-58: USAAC BT-14 with stressed-skin fuselage, 336-kW (450-hp) R-985-25 Wasp Junior, BC-1A outer wings and tail, 251 built of which 27 were re-engined in 1941 with 298-kW (400-hp) R-985-11 as BT-14A
NA-20 (NA-16-2H): R-1340-engined NA-18, sold to Honduras
NA-31 (NA-16-4M): as BT-9 with 336-kW (450-hp) R-975-E3, one sold to Sweden with licence to ASJA, see licence production below
NA-32 (NA-16-1A): two pattern aircraft sold with licence in 1937 to Commonwealth Aircraft (Australia); as NA-26 (see below) but fixed landing gear
NA-34 (NA-16-4P): for Argentina, two nose and one dorsal guns, full radio, bomb racks, 30 built
NA-37 (NA-16-4R): demonstrator for Japan, 336-kW (450-hp) R-985-9CG, three-bladed propeller, via Mitsubishi to Imperial Japanese Navy as KXA1
NA-38 (NA-16-4M): one NA-31 supplied in kit form to Sweden
NA-41 (NA-16-4C): as BT-9C with R-975 for China, 35 built
NA-42 (NA-16-2A): as NA-20 plus nose/dorsal guns, two to Honduras
NA-46 (NA-16-4): as BT-9C plus two guns, bomb racks under centre section, R-975, 12 for Brazilian navy
NA-47 (NA-16-4RW): as NA-37 but R-975-E3 with two-bladed propeller, supplied as kit to Imperial Japanese Navy, became KXA2
NA-56: new BC-1A airframe but fixed gear, 448-kW (600-hp) R-1340, 50 for China
NA-57: as NA-23 for French Armée de l'Air (200) and Aéronavale (30); 214 on strength of Luftwaffe, Vichy French air force 1941

NA-64: as NA-57 but new BC-1A wings and tail; for Armée de l'Air (200) and Aéronavale (30), but at 111th delivery France fell and other 119 diverted to RAF and passed on as Yale Mk I to RCAF as wireless (radio) trainer
NA-26: first of retractable-gear family, 448-kW (600-hp) R-1340, combat equipment, one demonstrator evaluated by USAAC as BT-9D
NA-27 (NA-16-2H): European demonstrator as NA-26, sold to Fokker with licence as PH-APG, later air force no. 997, destroyed 11 May 1940
NA-33 (NA-16-2K): second pattern for CAC (Australia), see licence production below
NA-36: USAAC BC-1, armament, 448-kW (600-hp) R-1340-7 or -47, 150 built, plus 30 BC-1I instrument trainers; last three completed as NA-54
NA-45 (NA-16-1GV): as BC-1, three for Venezuela
NA-48 (NA-16-3C): as BC-1, 15 for China
NA-49 (NA-16-1E): as BC-1 but British equipment, usually unarmed, 400 for RAF as Harvard Mk I (first US aircraft bought for RAF)
NA-52: SNJ-1 for USN, as BC-1 but stressed-skin fuselage and integral tanks, 16 built
NA-54: last three BC-1 completed with redesigned outer wings and rudder to speed production, also R-1340-45 with three-bladed propeller, stressed-skin fuselage, integral tanks
NA-55: USAAC BC-1A, as BC-1 but new wings and tail and stressed-skin fuselage, 29 for National Guard and 54 for USAAC Reserve, plus nine more completed as AT-6
NA-59: continuation of BC-1A under new designation AT-6, total 94 including nine ordered as NA-55
NA-61: (NA-16-1E): as NA-49 but for RCAF, 30 built
NA-65: USN, as NA-52 but R-1340-56 and controllable-pitch propeller, 36 built as SNJ-2
NA-66: NA-59 with British equipment as Harvard Mk II with R-1340-49, 600 built, 20 RAF, 67 RNZAF, 511 assigned RCAF but 486 delivered
NA-71: (NA-16-3): as NA-59, three for Venezuela
NA-75: as NA-66, Harvard Mk II, 100 for RCAF
NA-76: as NA-66, order for 450 for Armée de l'Air placed June 1940 two weeks before capitulation, all taken over by RAF as Harvard Mk II, of which 259 to RCAF
NA-77: as NA-59 with removable fuel tanks and R-1340-9, 517 for US Army as AT-6A plus 120 for US Navy as ANJ-3
NA-78: as NA-77 but built at new Dallas plant, 1,130 AT-6A plus 150 SNJ-3
NA-79: further (1940) contract for 25 SNJ-2
NA-81: Harvard Mk II as NA-66, 24 for RAF, 101 for RCAF
NA-84: as NA-77 but R-1340-AN-1 and one 7.62-mm (0.3-in) dorsal gun (in other AT-6s merely provision for this); AT-6B gunnery trainer, 400 from Dallas
NA-88: as NA-84 but extensive substitutes for aluminium in AT-6C and SNJ-4; during run, decision to revert to original structure but switch to 24-volt electrics, still as NA-88 but with US Army/US Navy designations AT-6D/SNJ-5; totals, all from Dallas, 9,331 comprising 2,970 AT-6Cs (of which 726 to RAF as Harvard Mk IIA), 2,400 SNJ-4s, 2,604 AT-6Ds (351 to RAF as Harvard Mk III), and 1,357 SNJ-5s
NA-119: standard AT-6Ds supplied to Brazil in 1944 as 10 assembled airframes, 10 sets of major airframe sections and 61 in kit form for completion by Construcciones Aeronauticas SA
NA-121: final batch of 800 AT-6Ds plus 956 AT-6Fs with redesigned outer wings and rear fuselage for sustained six-*g* manoeuvres and clear-view rear canopy; 411 (not, as often reported, 931) AT-6Fs transferred to USN as SNJ-6s
NA-168: first major post-war contract for remanufacture of NA-88 to T-6G standard with updated cockpit, new avionics, steerable tailwheel, modified main gears, extended fuel capacity, square-tip propeller (with spinner, often removed in service) and AN-1 series engine; this batch, 691 for USAF (serials 49-2897/3536 and 50-1317/1326), plus 59 LT-6Gs equipped for FAC duties in Korea (49-3537/3596)
NA-182: further batches of remanufactured T-6Gs, total 824 (51-14314/15137)
NA-186: design data for T-6J provided to CCF (see licence production)
NA-188: further remanufactured T-6Gs, total 107 (51-15138/15237 and -16071/16077)
NA-195: more T-6Gs, total 11 (51-17354/17364)
NA-197: June 1952, last T-6G remanufacture contract, total 110 (52-8197/8246, 53-4555/4614)
Many T-6G blocks were assigned to friendly air forces under MDAP, and numerous other wartime aircraft were modified without NA type numbers, examples being the AT-6D re-engined with 373-kW (500-hp) Ranger V-770-9 as XAT-6E, the USN SNJ-3Cs, -4Cs and -5Cs with hooks for carrier training, the AT-6Fs rebuilt by the USAF as T-6Fs for front-line observation in Korea, and the large numbers of USN aircraft (mainly SNJ-4s) remanufactured at NAS Pensacola in 1951-53 to approximately T-6G standard with designation SNJ-7 and (armed) SNJ-7B. NAA's contract for 240 NA-198 (Navy SNJ-8) new aircraft to similar standard was cancelled

NAA Attack variants

NA-44: prototype attack model with 586-kW (785-hp) Wright R-1820-F52 Cyclone, stressed-skin throughout, two wing guns, two cowl guns, one (optional 12.7-mm/0.5-in) in rear cockpit and 181-kg (400-lb) bombload; prototype became No. 3344 of RCAF, served to 1947
NA-69: batch of 10 for Siam, requisitioned by USAAC and put into combat duty in Philippines as A-27s (41-18890/18899)
NA-72: batch of 30 delivered to Brazil
NA-74: batch of 12 for Chile

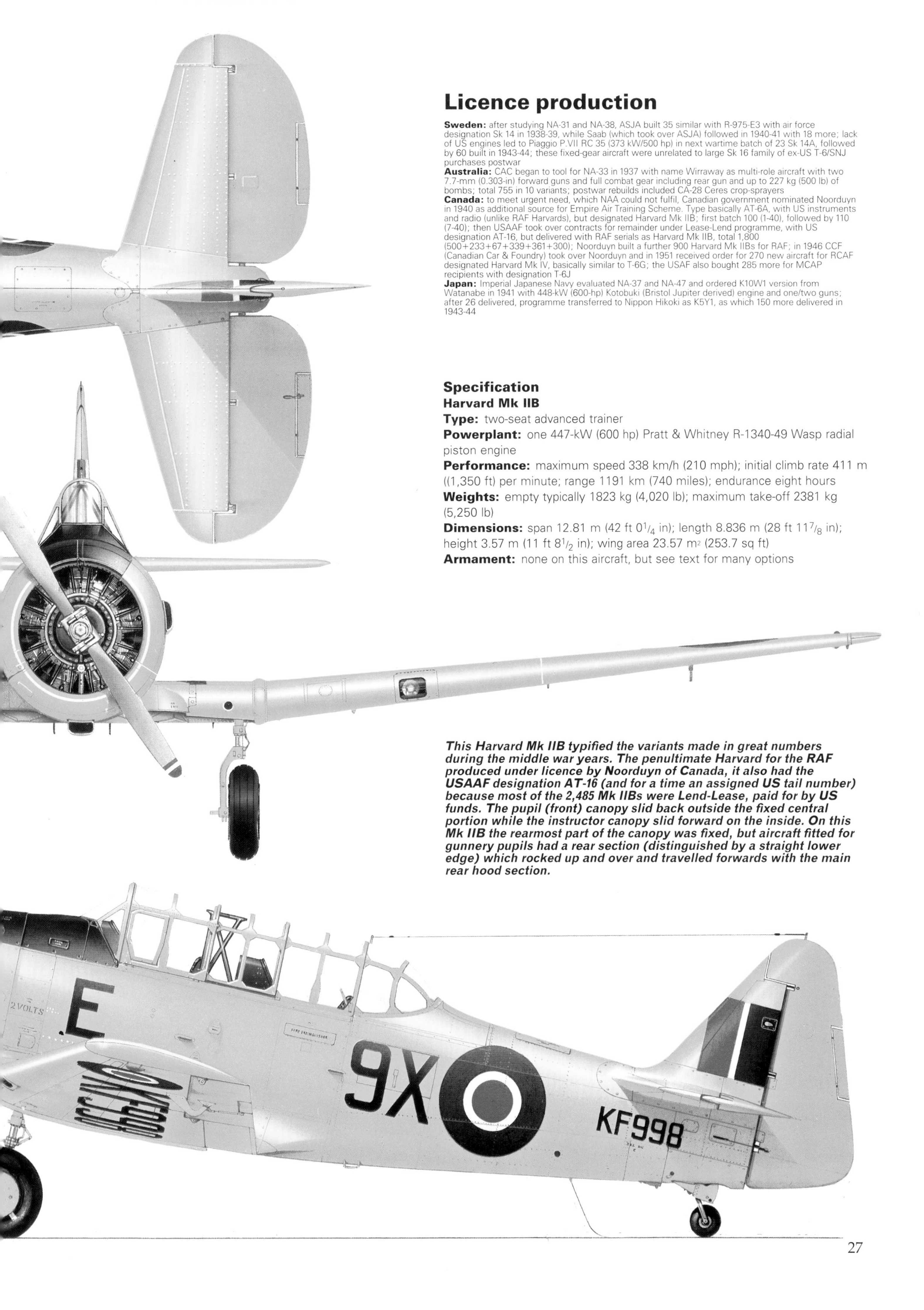

Licence production

Sweden: after studying NA-31 and NA-38, ASJA built 35 similar with R-975-E3 with air force designation Sk 14 in 1938-39, while Saab (which took over ASJA) followed in 1940-41 with 18 more; lack of US engines led to Piaggio P.VII RC 35 (373 kW/500 hp) in next wartime batch of 23 Sk 14A, followed by 60 built in 1943-44; these fixed-gear aircraft were unrelated to large Sk 16 family of ex-US T-6/SNJ purchases postwar
Australia: CAC began to tool for NA-33 in 1937 with name Wirraway as multi-role aircraft with two 7.7-mm (0.303-in) forward guns and full combat gear including rear gun and up to 227 kg (500 lb) of bombs; total 755 in 10 variants; postwar rebuilds included CA-28 Ceres crop-sprayers
Canada: to meet urgent need, which NAA could not fulfil, Canadian government nominated Noorduyn in 1940 as additional source for Empire Air Training Scheme. Type basically AT-6A, with US instruments and radio (unlike RAF Harvards), but designated Harvard Mk IIB; first batch 100 (1-40), followed by 110 (7-40); then USAAF took over contracts for remainder under Lease-Lend programme, with US designation AT-16, but delivered with RAF serials as Harvard Mk IIB, total 1,800 (500+233+67+339+361+300); Noorduyn built a further 900 Harvard Mk IIBs for RAF; in 1946 CCF (Canadian Car & Foundry) took over Noorduyn and in 1951 received order for 270 new aircraft for RCAF designated Harvard Mk IV, basically similar to T-6G; the USAF also bought 285 more for MCAP recipients with designation T-6J
Japan: Imperial Japanese Navy evaluated NA-37 and NA-47 and ordered K10W1 version from Watanabe in 1941 with 448-kW (600-hp) Kotobuki (Bristol Jupiter derived) engine and one/two guns; after 26 delivered, programme transferred to Nippon Hikoki as K5Y1, as which 150 more delivered in 1943-44

Specification

Harvard Mk IIB

Type: two-seat advanced trainer
Powerplant: one 447-kW (600 hp) Pratt & Whitney R-1340-49 Wasp radial piston engine
Performance: maximum speed 338 km/h (210 mph); initial climb rate 411 m ((1,350 ft) per minute; range 1191 km (740 miles); endurance eight hours
Weights: empty typically 1823 kg (4,020 lb); maximum take-off 2381 kg (5,250 lb)
Dimensions: span 12.81 m (42 ft 0$^1/_4$ in); length 8.836 m (28 ft 11$^7/_8$ in); height 3.57 m (11 ft 8$^1/_2$ in); wing area 23.57 m^2 (253.7 sq ft)
Armament: none on this aircraft, but see text for many options

This Harvard Mk IIB typified the variants made in great numbers during the middle war years. The penultimate Harvard for the RAF produced under licence by Noorduyn of Canada, it also had the USAAF designation AT-16 (and for a time an assigned US tail number) because most of the 2,485 Mk IIBs were Lend-Lease, paid for by US funds. The pupil (front) canopy slid back outside the fixed central portion while the instructor canopy slid forward on the inside. On this Mk IIB the rearmost part of the canopy was fixed, but aircraft fitted for gunnery pupils had a rear section (distinguished by a straight lower edge) which rocked up and over and travelled forwards with the main rear hood section.

Fieseler Fi 156C

Specification
Fieseler Fi 156C series

Type: STOL liaison, observation and rescue aircraft
Powerplant: one 179-kW (240-hp) Argus As 10C-3 inverted V-8 air-cooled piston engine
Performance: maximum speed 175 km/h (109 mph); cruising speed 130 km/h (81 mph); range (standard wing fuel) 467 km (290 miles)
Weights: empty 930 kg (2,050 lb); normal loaded 1325 kg (2,920 lb)
Dimensions: span 14.25 m (46 ft 9 in); length 9.9 m (32 ft 5.76 in); height 3.0 m (10 ft 0 in); wing area 26.0 m^2 (279.86 sq ft)
Armament: provision for one 7.92-mm (0.312-in) MG15 machine-gun with four spare 75-round magazines.

Fieseler Storch variants

Fi 156 B: projected variants with movable leading-edge slats; not built
Fi 156C-0: pre-production version of an improved Fi 156A-1 with raised rear-cabin glazing to allow installation of a rear-firing 7.92-mm (0.31-in) machine-gun
Fi 156B-1: liaison and staff transport version
Fi 156C-2: reconnaissance version with one camera and two-man crew; some late examples equipped to carry one stretcher for casualty evacuation
Fi 156C-3: general-purpose version, some with improved Argus As 10P engine
Fi 156C-3/Trop: tropicalised version of the Fi 156C-3 with engine dust/sand filters
Fi 156C-5: similar to 156C-3 but with Argus As 10P engine as standard and provision to carry an underfuselage drop tank or camera installation
Fi 156C-5/Trop: tropicalised version of the above
Fi 156D-0: pre-production ambulance version with improved accommodation for one stretcher and an enlarged loading/unloading hatch; powered by Argus As 10C engine
Fi 156D-1: production version of the above with Argus As 10P engine as standard
Fi 156E-0: designation of 10 pre-production aircraft with a form of tracked landing gear, the main units each with two wheels in tandem linked by pneumatic rubber track; no further production
Fi 256: two examples only of larger capacity (5-seat) civil version, built at Morane-Saulnier factory at Puteaux, France, during 1943-44

Without doubt the Fieseler Storch was the prime example of an army co-operation and observation aircraft, and certainly the design by which other types operating in these roles were judged. This view of an Fi 156C-3 clearly illustrates the purposeful design of the undercarriage with the long compression legs incorporating long-stroke, oil-damping shock absorbers of high vertical descent rates. Such was the success of the Storch in its intended role that trials were conducted around supply-dropping, coastal patrol and light bombing roles, though only as secondary operations.

Heinkel He 111H-16

Specification
Heinkel He 111H-16

Type: five-seat medium night bomber/pathfinder and glider tug
Powerplant: two 1006-kW (1,350-hp) Junkers Jumo 211F-2 inline piston engines
Performance: maximum speed 435 km/h (270 mph) at 600 m (19,685 ft); service ceiling 8500 m (27,890 ft); normal range 1950 km (1,212 miles)
Weights: empty 8680 kg (19,136 lb); maximum take-off 14000 kg (30,864 lb)
Dimensions: span 22.60 m (74 ft 1¾ in); length 16.40 m (53 ft 9½ in); height 4.00 m (13 ft 1¼ in); wing area 86.50 m^2 (931.1 sq ft)
Armament: one 20-mm MG FF cannon, one 13-mm (0.51-in) MG 131 and up to seven 7.92-mm (0.31-in) MG 15 and MG 81 machine-guns, plus one 2000-kg (4,409-lb) bomb carried externally and one 500-kg (1,102-lb) bomb internally, or eight 250-kg (551-kg) bombs all internally

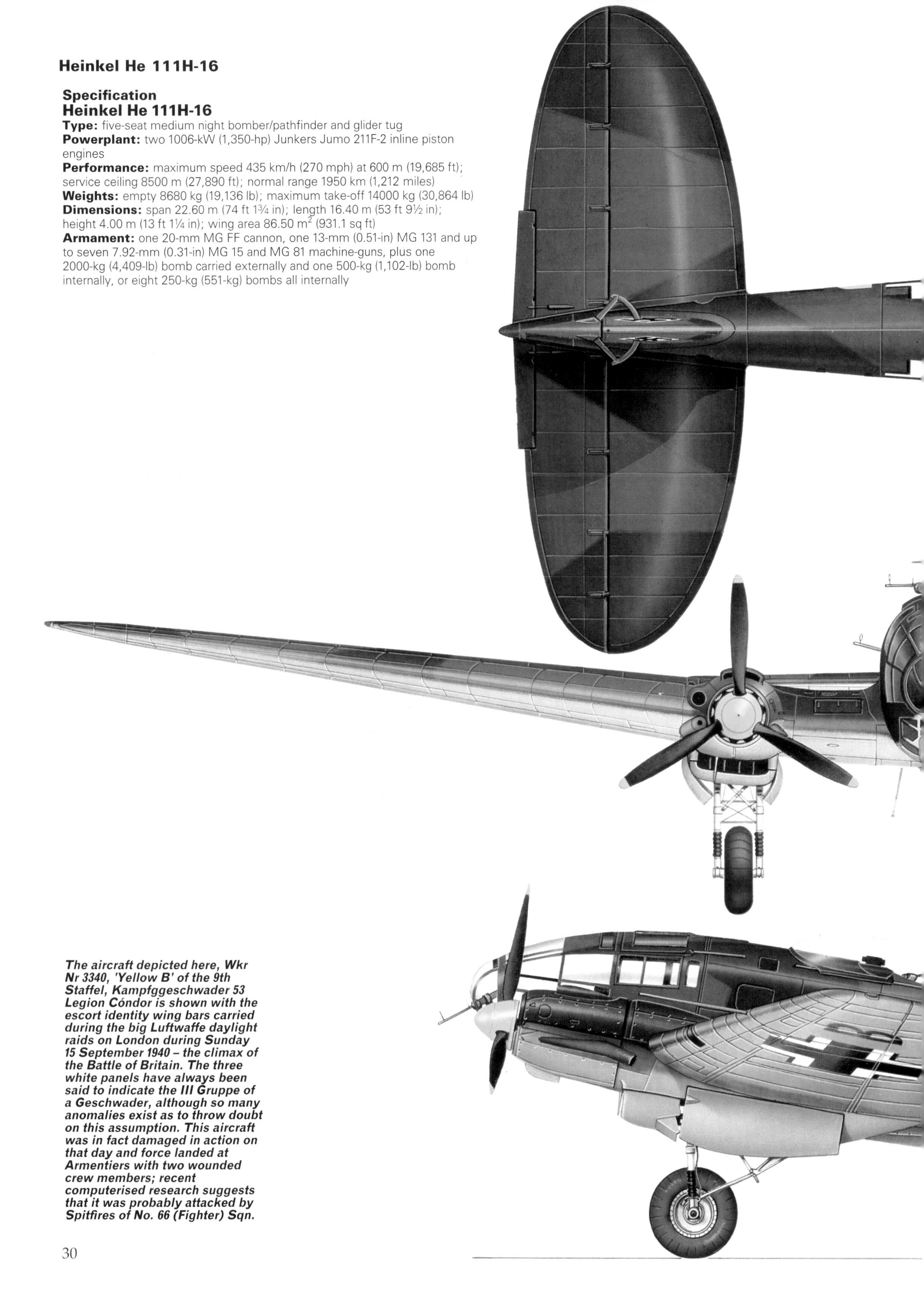

The aircraft depicted here, Wkr Nr 3340, 'Yellow B' of the 9th Staffel, Kampfggeschwader 53 Legion Cóndor is shown with the escort identity wing bars carried during the big Luftwaffe daylight raids on London during Sunday 15 September 1940 – the climax of the Battle of Britain. The three white panels have always been said to indicate the III Gruppe of a Geschwader, although so many anomalies exist as to throw doubt on this assumption. This aircraft was in fact damaged in action on that day and force landed at Armentiers with two wounded crew members; recent computerised research suggests that it was probably attacked by Spitfires of No. 66 (Fighter) Sqn.

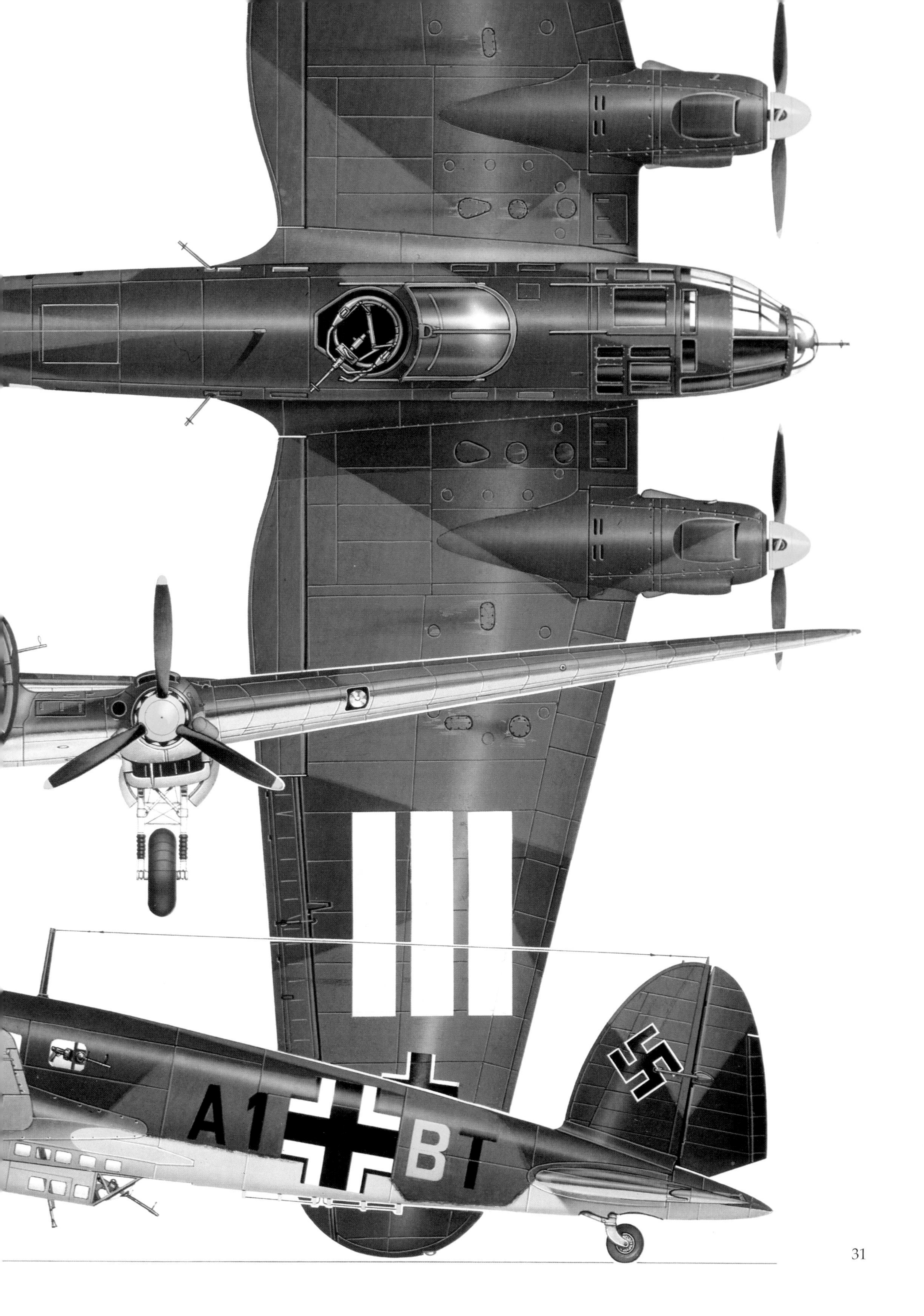
A1 BT

T4638
F

Specification
Bristol Beaufighter TF.Mk X
Type: two-seat anti-shipping strike fighter
Powerplant: two 1294-kW (1,735-hp) Bristol Hercules XVII sleeve-valve radial engines
Performance: maximum speed 488 km/h (303 mph) at 400 m (1,300 ft); climb to 1525 m (5,000 ft) in 3 minutes 30 seconds; service ceiling 4575 m (15,000 ft); normal range 2367 km (1,470 miles)
Weights: empty 7082 kg (15,600 lb); maximum take-off 11441 kg (25,200 lb)
Dimensions: span 17.64 m (57 ft 10 in); length 12.71 m (41 ft 8 in); height 4.83 m (15 ft 10 in); wing area 47.13 m^2 (503 sq ft)
Armament: four nose-mounted 20-mm cannon and one rear 7.7-mm (0.303-in) machine-gun, plus one 750-kg (1,650-lb) or 966-kg (2,127-lb) torpedo, or eight 27-kg (60-lb) rockets and two 113-kg (250-lb) bombs under the wings

T4638 was the 16th Bristol Beaufighter Mk IF night-fighter built by the Fairey Aviation Company; equipped with AI Mk IV, characterised by the broad arrow nose aerial and outer wing arrays, and carrying an armament of four 20-mm and six 7.7-mm (0.303-in) guns, T4638 joined No. 604 (County of Middlesex) Squadron at Middle Wallop in 1941. At this time the squadron, commanded by Wing Commander John Cunningham, was the top-scoring night-fighter unit in the RAF, and had been one of the first to receive the Beaufighter at the height of the Battle of Britain in September 1940. Although crews had been slow to master the use of AI radar, by the end of the German night blitz of 1940-1 the Beaufighter had become the world's most effective night-fighter.

Messerschmitt Bf 109E-7

Introduced into Luftwaffe service midway through the Battle of Britain in August 1940, the Messerschmitt Bf 109E-7 featured a modified fuel system and attachments for a ventral drop tank. Being equipped to carry the extra fuel, the new aircraft were able to provide effective escort for the big daylight raids over London in September 1940. 'Red 2' (no. 2058), depicted here, was being flown by Unteroffizier Klick of 3./LG 2 when it was shot down by RAF fighters in the famous raids on London of 15 September.

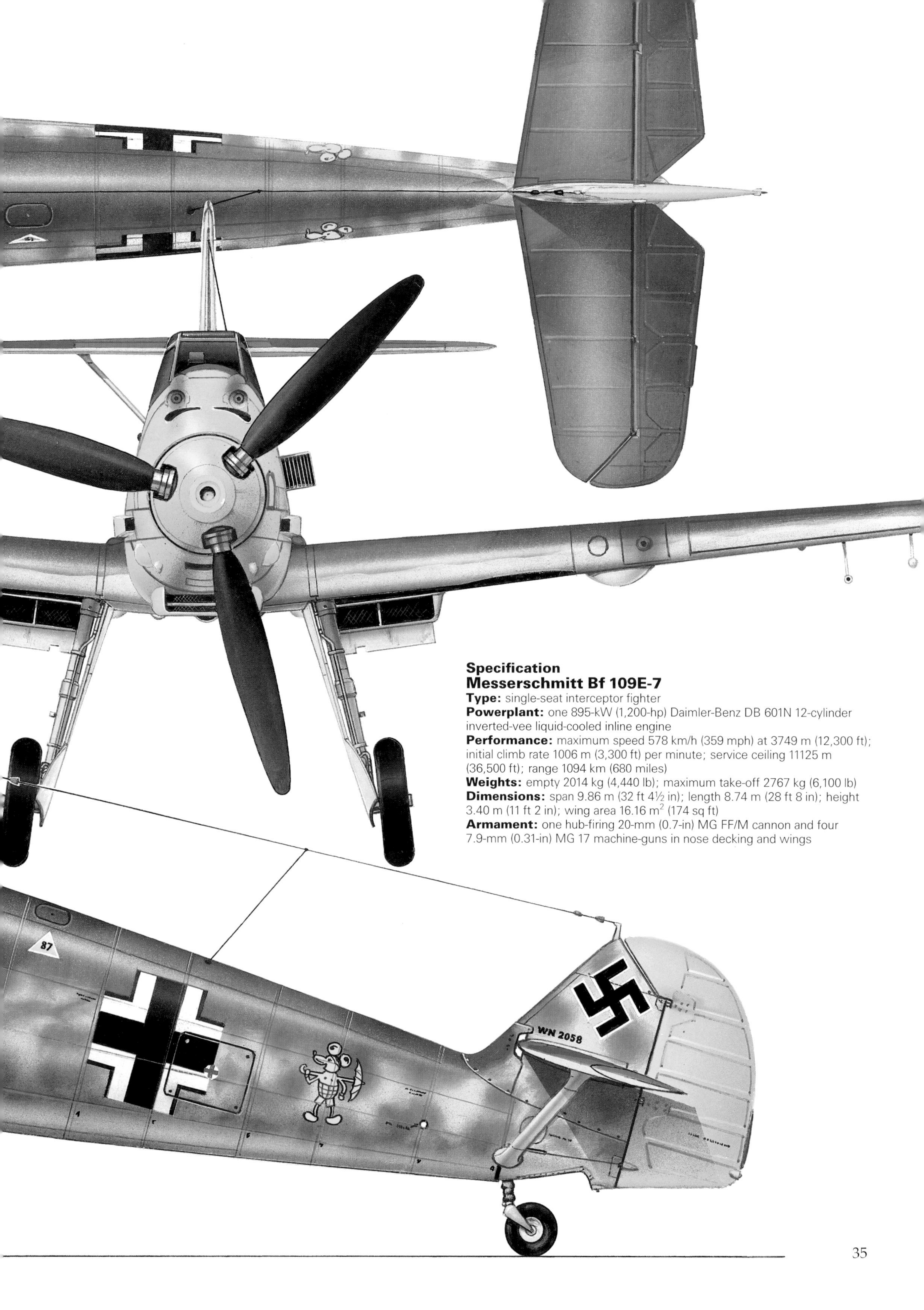

Specification
Messerschmitt Bf 109E-7
Type: single-seat interceptor fighter
Powerplant: one 895-kW (1,200-hp) Daimler-Benz DB 601N 12-cylinder inverted-vee liquid-cooled inline engine
Performance: maximum speed 578 km/h (359 mph) at 3749 m (12,300 ft); initial climb rate 1006 m (3,300 ft) per minute; service ceiling 11125 m (36,500 ft); range 1094 km (680 miles)
Weights: empty 2014 kg (4,440 lb); maximum take-off 2767 kg (6,100 lb)
Dimensions: span 9.86 m (32 ft 4½ in); length 8.74 m (28 ft 8 in); height 3.40 m (11 ft 2 in); wing area 16.16 m^2 (174 sq ft)
Armament: one hub-firing 20-mm (0.7-in) MG FF/M cannon and four 7.9-mm (0.31-in) MG 17 machine-guns in nose decking and wings

Short S.25 Sunderland III

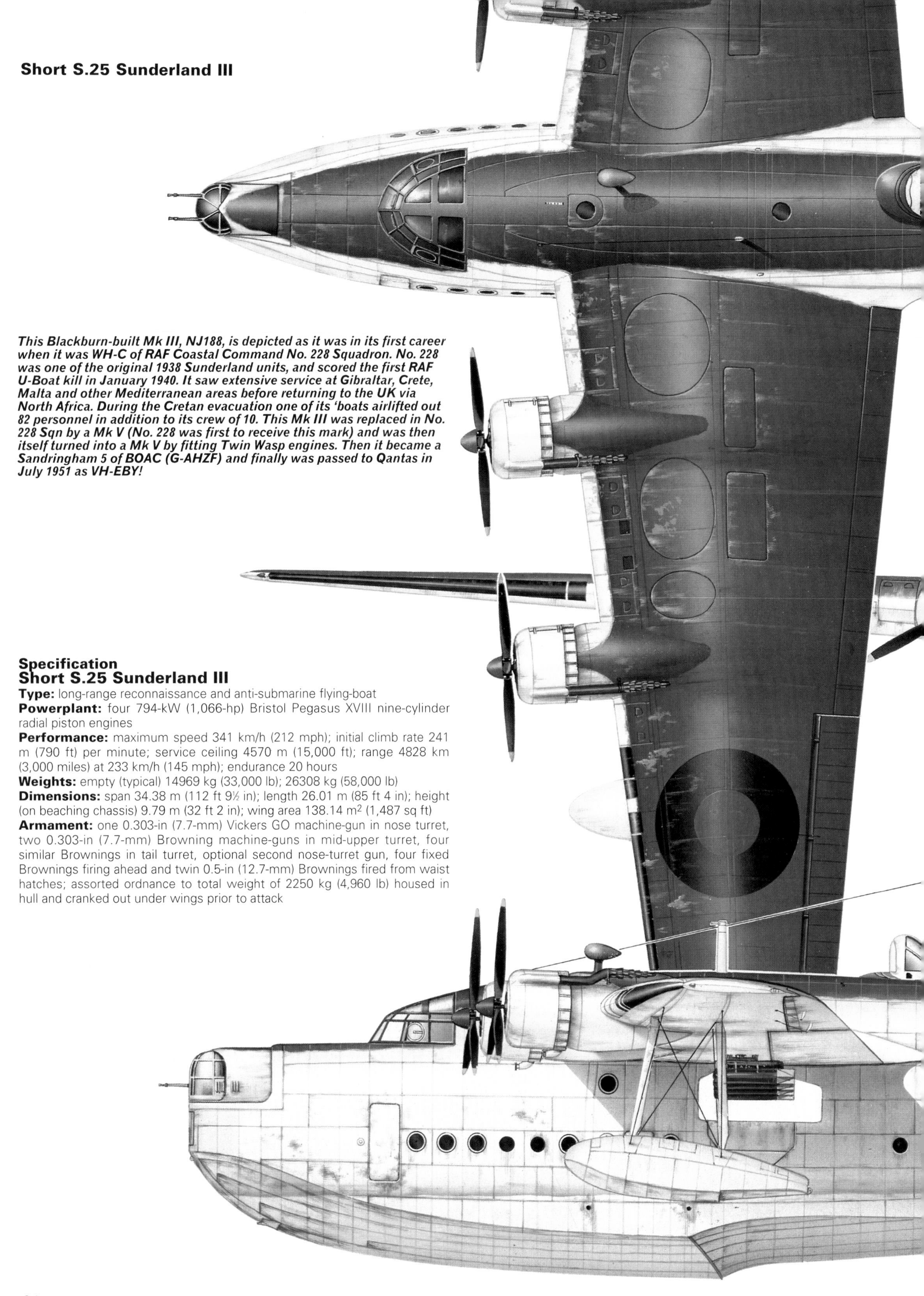

This Blackburn-built Mk III, NJ188, is depicted as it was in its first career when it was WH-C of RAF Coastal Command No. 228 Squadron. No. 228 was one of the original 1938 Sunderland units, and scored the first RAF U-Boat kill in January 1940. It saw extensive service at Gibraltar, Crete, Malta and other Mediterranean areas before returning to the UK via North Africa. During the Cretan evacuation one of its 'boats airlifted out 82 personnel in addition to its crew of 10. This Mk III was replaced in No. 228 Sqn by a Mk V (No. 228 was first to receive this mark) and was then itself turned into a Mk V by fitting Twin Wasp engines. Then it became a Sandringham 5 of BOAC (G-AHZF) and finally was passed to Qantas in July 1951 as VH-EBY!

Specification
Short S.25 Sunderland III

Type: long-range reconnaissance and anti-submarine flying-boat
Powerplant: four 794-kW (1,066-hp) Bristol Pegasus XVIII nine-cylinder radial piston engines
Performance: maximum speed 341 km/h (212 mph); initial climb rate 241 m (790 ft) per minute; service ceiling 4570 m (15,000 ft); range 4828 km (3,000 miles) at 233 km/h (145 mph); endurance 20 hours
Weights: empty (typical) 14969 kg (33,000 lb); 26308 kg (58,000 lb)
Dimensions: span 34.38 m (112 ft 9½ in); length 26.01 m (85 ft 4 in); height (on beaching chassis) 9.79 m (32 ft 2 in); wing area 138.14 m^2 (1,487 sq ft)
Armament: one 0.303-in (7.7-mm) Vickers GO machine-gun in nose turret, two 0.303-in (7.7-mm) Browning machine-guns in mid-upper turret, four similar Brownings in tail turret, optional second nose-turret gun, four fixed Brownings firing ahead and twin 0.5-in (12.7-mm) Brownings fired from waist hatches; assorted ordnance to total weight of 2250 kg (4,960 lb) housed in hull and cranked out under wings prior to attack

NJ188
VH C

Hawker Hurricane Mk I

Specification
Hawker Hurricane Mk I

Type: single-seat interceptor fighter
Powerplant: one 768-kW (1,030-hp) Rolls-Royce Merlin III inline piston engine
Performance: maximum speed 511 km/h (318 mph) at 5500 m (18,000 ft); initial climb rate 770 m (2,520 ft) per minute; service ceiling 10970 m (36,000 ft); maximum range 740 km (460 miles)
Weights: empty 2118 kg (4,670 lb); maximum take-off 2994 kg (6,600 lb)
Dimensions: span 12.20 m (40 ft 0 in); length 9.59 m (31 ft 4 in); height 3.96 m (12 ft 11½ in); wing area 23.93 m^2 (257.6 sq ft)
Armament: eight 7.7-mm (0.303-in) Browning machine-guns with 2,660 rounds of ammunition

Representative of the classic RAF Battle of Britain Hurricane I, P3059 served with No. 501 (County of Gloucester) Squadron during August 1940. Aircraft of this Gloster Aircraft-produced batch, equipped from the outset with Rotol constant-speed propellers, started delivery to RAF fighter squadrons in May and continued throughout the Battle of Britain; it has been said that the Rotol propeller transformed the Hurricane's performance from 'disappointing' to one of 'acceptable mediocrity', and modified aircraft were certainly much sought after among squadrons equipped with aircraft having the older de Havilland two-position propeller.

ON
P3059

Messerschmitt Bf 110C-4

Messerschmitt Bf 110C-4/B of 9. Staffel, Zerstörergeschwader 26 'Horst Wessel', shown carrying two 250-kg (551-lb) and four 100-kg (220-lb) bombs. This unit was among the first German units to be sent to the Mediterranean, being based at Palermo at the end of 1940.

Specification

Messerschmitt Bf 110C-4

Type: two-seat heavy fighter

Powerplant: two 821-kW (1,100-hp) Daimler-Benz DB 601A inverted V-12 piston engines

Performance: maximum speed 560 km/h (349 mph) at 7000 m (22,965 ft); initial climb rate 660 m (2,165 ft) per minute; service ceiling 10000 m (32,810 ft); normal range 775 km (482 miles)

Weights: empty 5200 kg (11,454 lb); maximum take-off 6750 kg (14,881 lb)

Dimensions: span 16.27 m (5 ft 3¾ in); length 12.65 m (41 ft 6¾ in); height 3.50 m (11 ft 6 in); wing area 38.40 m² (413.3 sq ft)

Armament: two 20-mm MG 151 cannon and four 7.92-mm (0.31-in) MG 17 guns in the nose firing forward, and one 7.92-mm (0.31-in) MG 812 twin gun on pivoted mounting in the rear cockpit firing aft

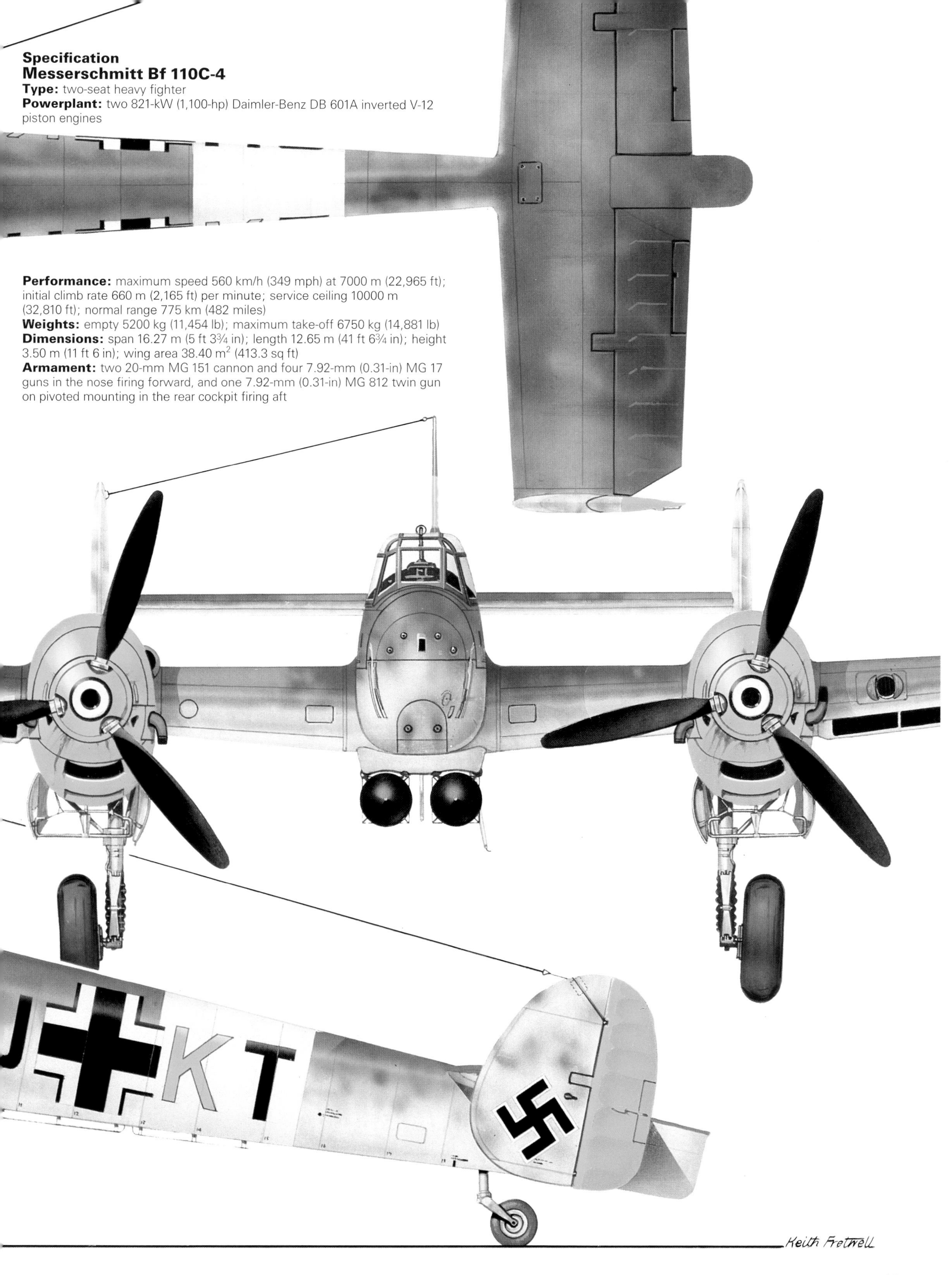

Halifax B.Mk I Series I

Specification
Halifax B.Mk I Series 1

Type: seven-seat heavy bomber
Powerplant: four 954-kW (1,280-hp) Rolls-Royce Merlin X V-12 engines
Performance: maximum speed 426 km/h (265 mph); service ceiling 6950 m (22,800 ft); initial climb 229 m (750 ft) per minute; range with 2631 kg (5,800 lb) bombload 3000 km (1,860 miles)
Weights: empty 15359 kg (33,860 lb); loaded 26308 kg (58,000 lb)
Dimensions: span 30.12 m (98 ft 10 in); length 21. 36 m (70 ft 1 in); height 6.32 m (20 ft 9 in); wing area 116 m^2 (1,250 sq ft)
Armament: normal bombload 5897 kg (13,000 lb) including mines or two torpedoes; (defensive) two 7.7-mm (0.303-in) Browning machine-guns in Boulton Paul nose turret, four in tail turret of same make, plus two Vickers 'K' machine-guns of same calibre aimed by hand through beam hatches

L9530 was one of the very first batch (L9485-9534) of production Halifaxes, delivered in the winter of 1940-41. Styled B.Mk I Series 1, it is shown after delivery to RAF No. 76 Sqn in Bomber Command's No. 4 Group at Middleton St George (today Tees-side Airport). The crest was applied by the pilot, Christopher Cheshire, brother of the more famous Leonard Cheshire who served with the first Halifax squadron, No. 35, and later went on to command No. 76. All bomb doors are shown open, and the projections aft of the trailing edge just outboard of the centre-section are fuel-jettison pipes. The 'acorn' carried above the fuselage, downstream of the navigator's astrodome, housed the rotatable direction-finding radio loop aerial.

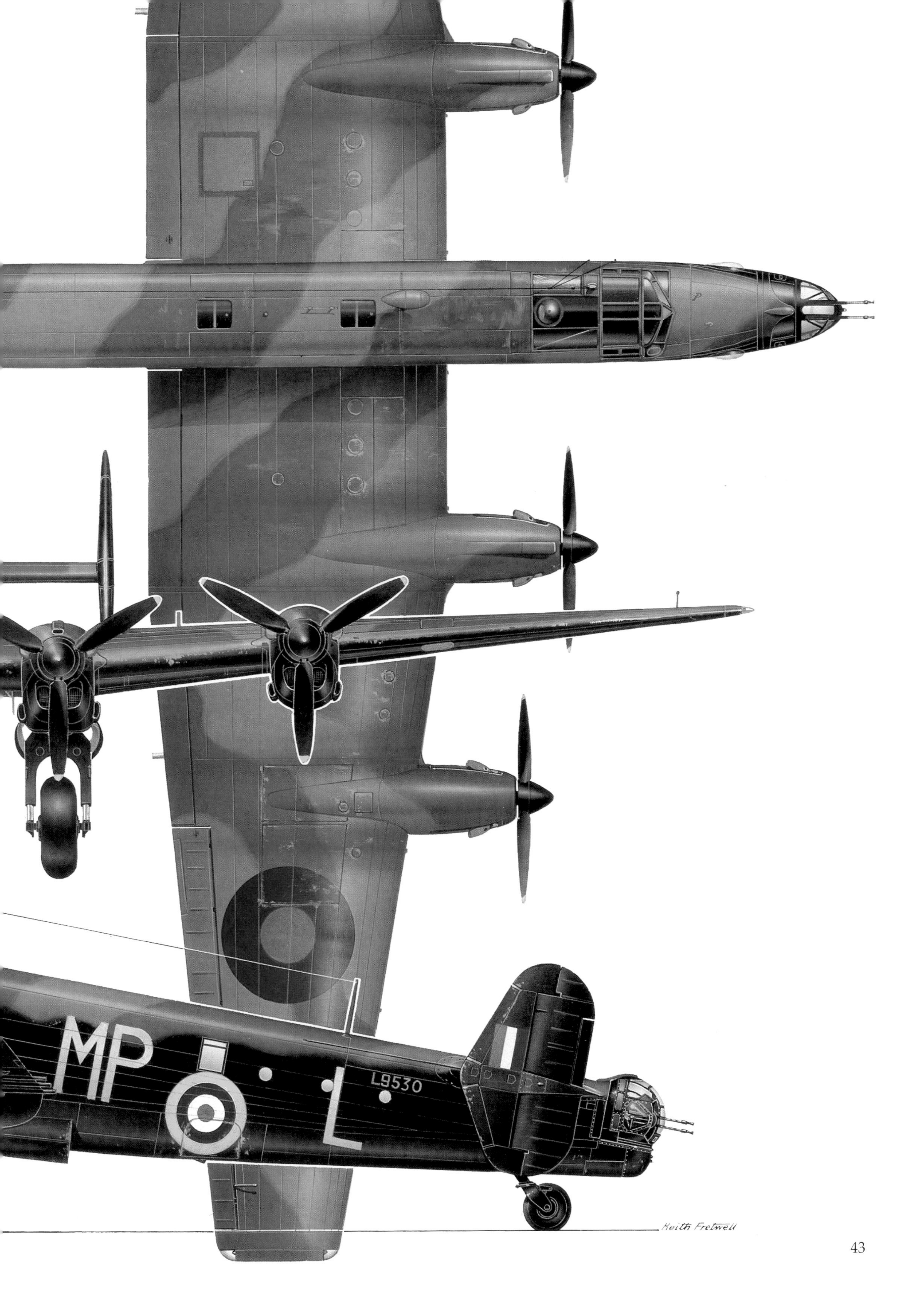
MP
L
L9530
Keith Fretwell

Junkers Ju 52/3mg7e

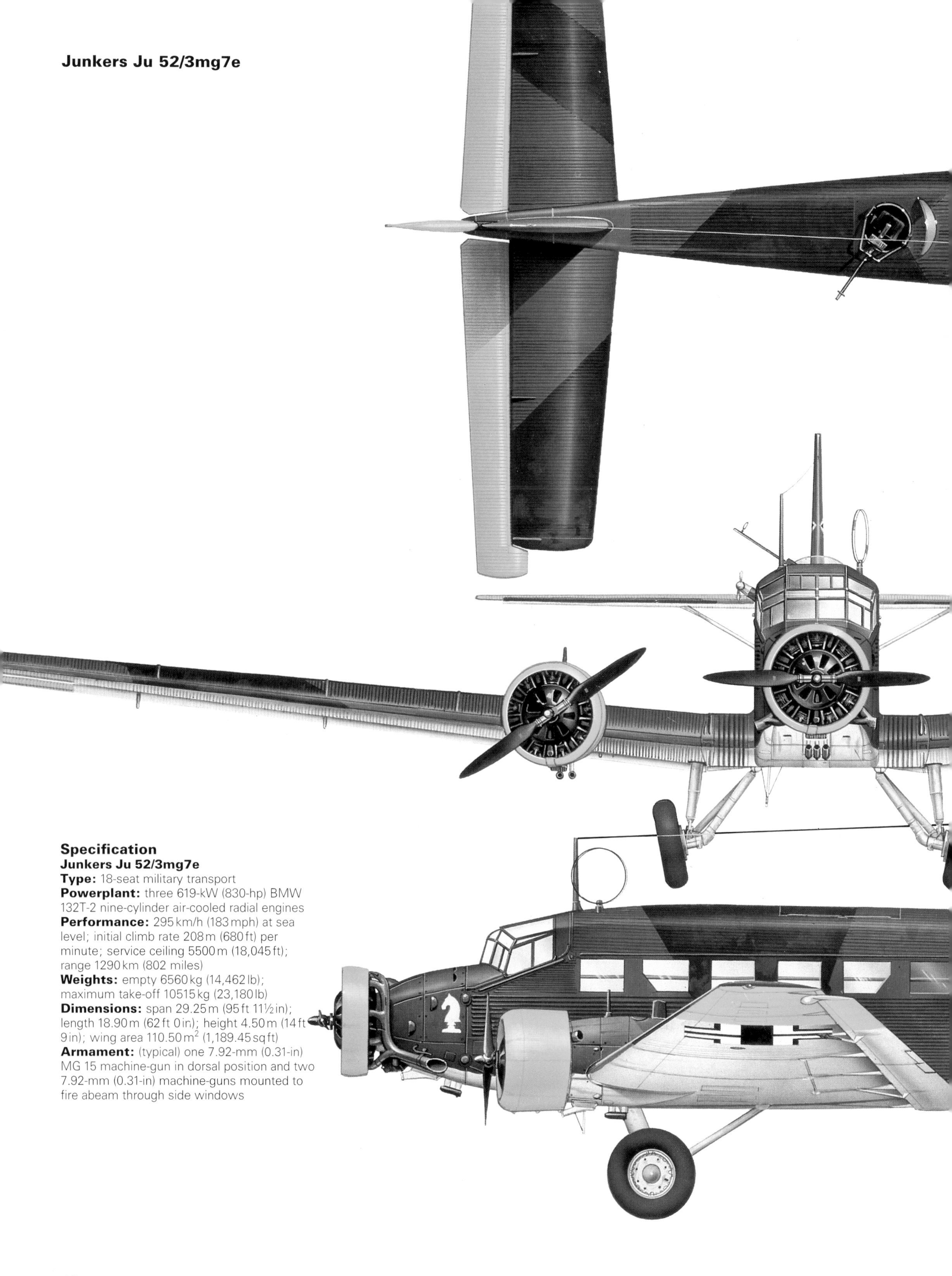

Specification

Junkers Ju 52/3mg7e
Type: 18-seat military transport
Powerplant: three 619-kW (830-hp) BMW 132T-2 nine-cylinder air-cooled radial engines
Performance: 295 km/h (183 mph) at sea level; initial climb rate 208 m (680 ft) per minute; service ceiling 5500 m (18,045 ft); range 1290 km (802 miles)
Weights: empty 6560 kg (14,462 lb); maximum take-off 10515 kg (23,180 lb)
Dimensions: span 29.25 m (95 ft 11½ in); length 18.90 m (62 ft 0 in); height 4.50 m (14 ft 9 in); wing area 110.50 m² (1,189.45 sq ft)
Armament: (typical) one 7.92-mm (0.31-in) MG 15 machine-gun in dorsal position and two 7.92-mm (0.31-in) machine-guns mounted to fire abeam through side windows

A Junkers Ju 52/3mg7e of 2.Staffel, KGrzbV 1, based at Milos, Greece, in May 1941 prior to the invasion of Crete. Under the command of Generalmajor Gerhard a fleet of 493 Ju 52/3ms was assembled for the landings, known as Operation 'Mercury', but owing to confusion over the island during the initial assault, subsequent waves of transports were delayed and the element of concentration was lost; of every four paratroopers dropped, one was killed or wounded. By the end of the operation more than 170 Ju 52/3ms had been lost or seriously damaged.

Vickers Wellington B.Mk III

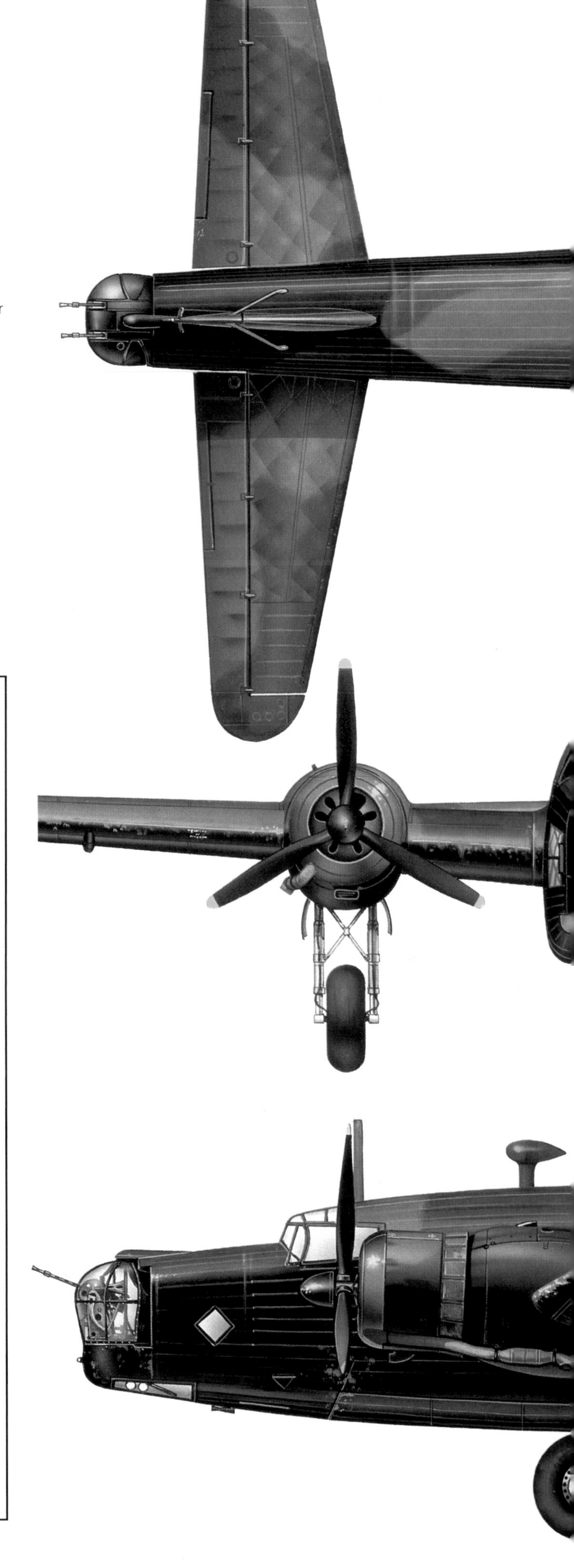

Specification
Vickers Wellington B.Mk III

Type: six-crew medium bomber
Powerplant: two 1119-kW (1,500-hp) Bristol Hercules XI air-cooled 14-cylinder radial piston engines
Performance: maximum speed 410 km/h (255 mph) at 3810 m (12,500 ft); initial climb rate 283 m (930 ft) per minute; service ceiling 5790 m (19,000 ft); range 3540 km (2,200 miles) with 680 kg (1,500 lb) of bombs, or 2478 km (1,540 miles) with 2041 kg (4,500 lb) of bombs
Weights: empty 8417 kg (18,556 lb); maximum take-off 13381 kg (29,500 lb)
Dimensions: span 26.26 m (86 ft 2 in); length 18.54 m (60 ft 10 in); height 5.31 m (17 ft 5 in); wing area 78.04 m^2 (840.0 sq ft)
Armament: two 7.7-mm (0.303-in) machine-guns in nose turret, four similar weapons in tail turret, and one similar weapon in each rear fuselage beam position, plus a maximum bombload of 2041 kg (4,500 lb), or one 1814-kg (4,000-lb) bomb

Vickers Wellington variants

Type 271: B.9/32 first prototype (K4049) with Pegasus X; first flown 15 June 1936
Type 285 Wellington Mk I: prototype (L4212) with Pegasus X; flown 23 December 1937
Type 290 Wellington Mk I: production, 183 built at Weybridge (180) and Chester (3) with Pegasus XVIII; Vickers turrets and 'dustbin'
Type 408 Wellington Mk IA: production, 187 built at Weybridge and Chester with Pegasus XVIII; Nash and Thompson turrets and 'dustbin'
Type 416 Wellington Mk IC: production, 2,685 built at Weybridge (1,052), Chester (1,583) and Blackpool (50); **Type 423** covered conversion of all bombers to carry 4,000-lb (1814-kg) bomb; beam guns (no 'dustbin')
Type 298 Wellington Mk II: prototype (L4250) with Merlin X; first flown 3 March 1939
Type 406 Wellington B.Mk II: production, 400 built at Weybridge with Merlin X
Type 299 Wellington Mk III: prototypes, L4251 with Hercules HEISM, and P9238 with Hercules III
Type 417 Wellington B.Mk III: production, 1,517 built at Chester (737) and Blackpool (780) in 1941-43; fighter-towing experiments by Flight Refuelling
Type 410 Wellington Mk IV: prototype (R1220) with Pratt & Whitney Twin Wasp radials
Type 424 Wellington B.Mk IV: production, 220 built at Chester with Twin Wasps
Type 421 Wellington Mk V: first prototype (R3298) with Hercules III
Type 407 Wellington Mk V: second prototype (R3299) with Hercules VIII
Type 432 Wellington Mk VI: prototype (W5795) with Rolls-Royce Merlin (various)
Type 442 Wellington B.Mk VI: production, 63 built at Weybridge; Sperry bomb sight; **Type 449** covered **Wellington Mk VIG** production; two aircraft to No. 109 Sqn
Type 430 Wellington Mk VII: prototype (T2545) cancelled; Merlin XX; production of 150 aircraft also cancelled
Type 429 Wellington GR.Mk VIII: production, with Pegasus XVIII; 397 built at Weybridge; 58 fitted with Leigh Light; provision to carry AS weapons (some aircraft with provision for torpedoes)
Type 437 Wellington IX: one transport prototype (P2522) converted from Wellington Mk IA; Hercules XVI
Type 440 Wellington B.Mk X: production, 3,803 built at Chester (2,434) and Blackpool (1,369); Hercules XI/XVI; **Type 619** covered post-war conversion to **Wellington T.Mk 10;** RP468 fitted with tail boom radar as G-ALUH; some sold to France in 1946; six to Royal Hellenic air force in April 1946
Type 454 Wellington Mk XI: prototype (MP502) with ASV Mk II; Hercules VI/XVI; **Type 459** covered MP545 with ASV Mk III
Type 458 Wellington GR.Mk XI: production, 180 built at Weybridge (105) and Blackpool (75); ASV Mk III and Hercules VIU/XVI
Type 455 Wellington GR.Mk XII: production, 58 built at Weybridge (50) and Chester (8); Leigh Light, ASV Mk III and Hercules VI/XVI; some to France in 1946
Type 466 Wellington GR.Mk XIII: production, 844 built at Weybridge (42) and Blackpool (802); Hercules XVI
Type 467 Wellington GR.Mk XIV: production, 841 built at Weybridge (53), Chester (538) and Blackpool (250); Hercules XVI; many supplied to France between April 1944 and July 1945; some sold to France in 1946
Wellington C.Mk XV: service conversion of Wellington Mk IAs to troop transport (originally designated **Wellington C.Mk IA)**; accommodation for 18 troops
Wellington C.Mk XVI: service conversion of Wellington Mk ICs to troop transport (originally designated **Wellington C.Mk IC);** modification as for Wellington C.Mk XV
Type 487 Wellington T.Mk XVII: kits for service conversion to trainer with Mosquito-type AI radar; Hercules XVII
Type 490 Wellington T.Mk XVIII: production, 80 built at Blackpool plus conversion of some Wellington Mk XIs; Hercules XVI; Mosquito-type radar-equipped 'flying classroom'
Wellington T.Mk XIX: service conversion from Wellington Mk X to trainer
Type 416 Wellington (II): L4250 with experimental installation of 40-mm Vickers gun in dorsal position; Merlin X; also modified with twin fins
Type 418 Wellington DWI.Mk I: conversion of P2516 for mine detonation; Ford auxiliary power unit
Type 419 Wellington DWI.Mk II: conversion of L4356 for mine detonation; Gipsy Six auxiliary power unit
Type 435 Wellington Mk IC: conversion of T2977 to mount Turbinlite for comparison with Leigh Light
Type 439 Wellington Mk II: Z8416 with experimental installation of 40-mm Vickers gun in nose; Merlin X
Type 443 Wellington Mk V: W5816 with conversion to Hercules VIII testbed
Type 445 Wellington (II): Z8570/G as testbed for Whittle W2B/23 jet in tail; **Type 470** covered Wellington II W5389/G with Whittle W2B jet, and **Type 486** covered Wellington II W5518 with W2/700 jet
Type 478 Wellington Mk X: LN718 with trial installation of Hercules 100
Type 602 Wellington X: LN715 as engine testbed with two Rolls-Royce Dart turboprops
Type 638 Wellington X: NA 857 as engine testbed with Napier Naiads; not completed
Wellington III: X3268 with glider-towing clearance for Hadrian, Hotspur and Horsa

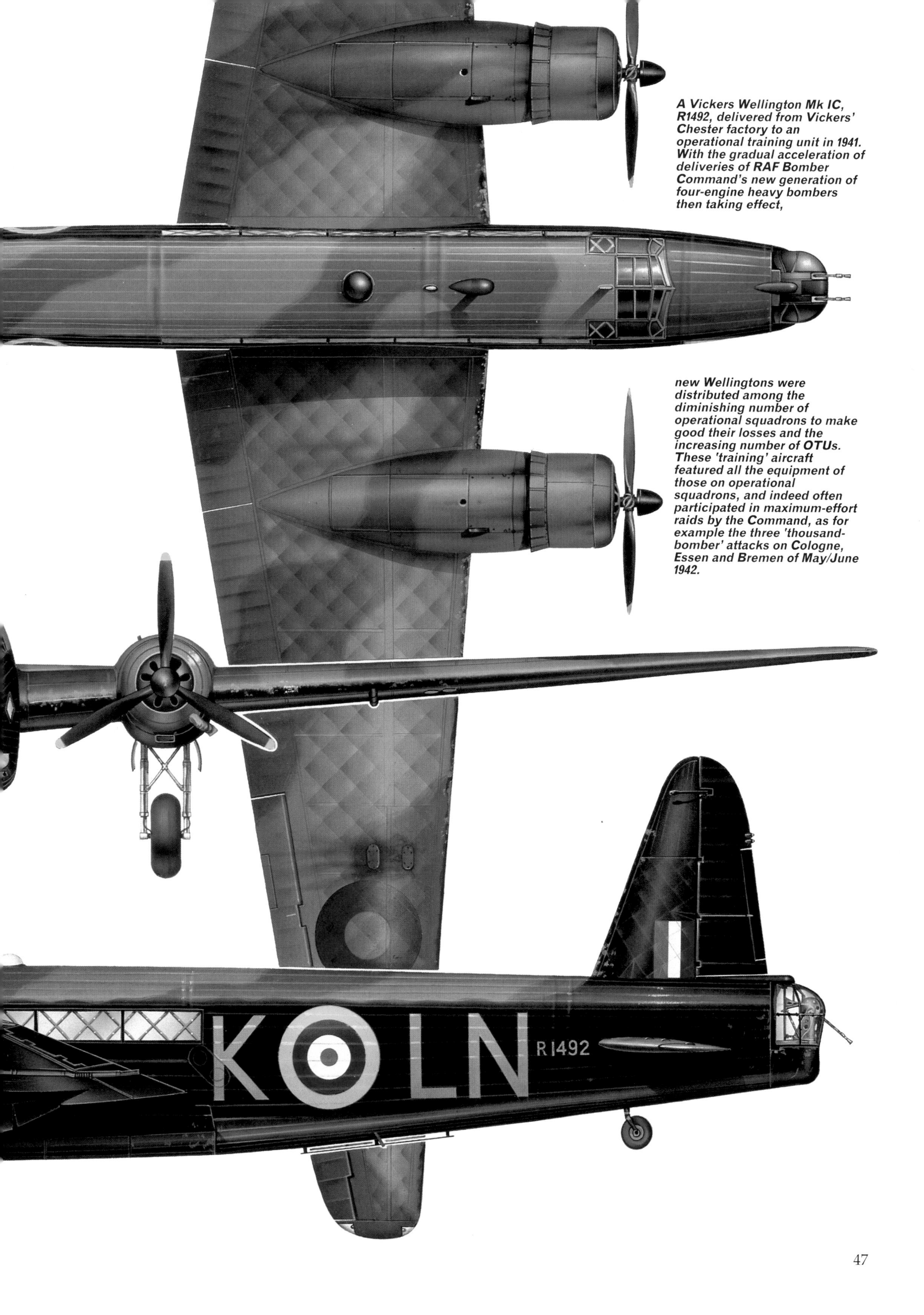

A Vickers Wellington Mk IC, R1492, delivered from Vickers' Chester factory to an operational training unit in 1941. With the gradual acceleration of deliveries of RAF Bomber Command's new generation of four-engine heavy bombers then taking effect, new Wellingtons were distributed among the diminishing number of operational squadrons to make good their losses and the increasing number of OTUs. These 'training' aircraft featured all the equipment of those on operational squadrons, and indeed often participated in maximum-effort raids by the Command, as for example the three 'thousand-bomber' attacks on Cologne, Essen and Bremen of May/June 1942.

Grumman TBF-1 Avenger

This drawing depicts one of the first TBF-1s to come off the line at Bethpage in early 1942. Only about 200 were delivered with the national insignia as shown, a red border with white rectangles being added in June 1943. The colour scheme of sea blue fading through grey to a white underside was introduced in 1943, all earlier TBFs having the original scheme of sea green above and light grey below. Other points of interest include the kinked steel main legs, fixed slots ahead of the fabric-covered ailerons, and crew door in the side of the rear fuselage.

Specification

Grumman TBF-1 Avenger

Type: three-seat carrier-based torpedo-bomber

Powerplant: one 1268-kW (1,700-hp) Wright R-2600-8 Cyclone 14-cylinder two-row radial piston engine

Performance: maximum speed 436 km/h (271 mph); typical long-range cruise 233 km/h (145 mph); range on internal fuel 1778 km (1,105 miles)

Weights: empty (TBF-1C) 4788 kg (10,555 lb); maximum loaded 7876 kg (17,364 lb)

Dimensions: span 16.51 m (54 ft 2 in); length 12.2 m (40 ft 0.2 in); height 4.19 m (13 ft 9 in); wing area 45.52 m^2 (490 sq ft)

Armament: one 7.62-mm (0.3-in) gun firing ahead (in TBF-1C, two 12.7-mm/0.5-in), one 12.7-mm (0.5-in) in turret and one 7.62-mm (0.3-in) in lower rear position; internal bay for one 577-mm (22.7-in) torpedo or up to 907 kg (2,000 lb) of other stores.

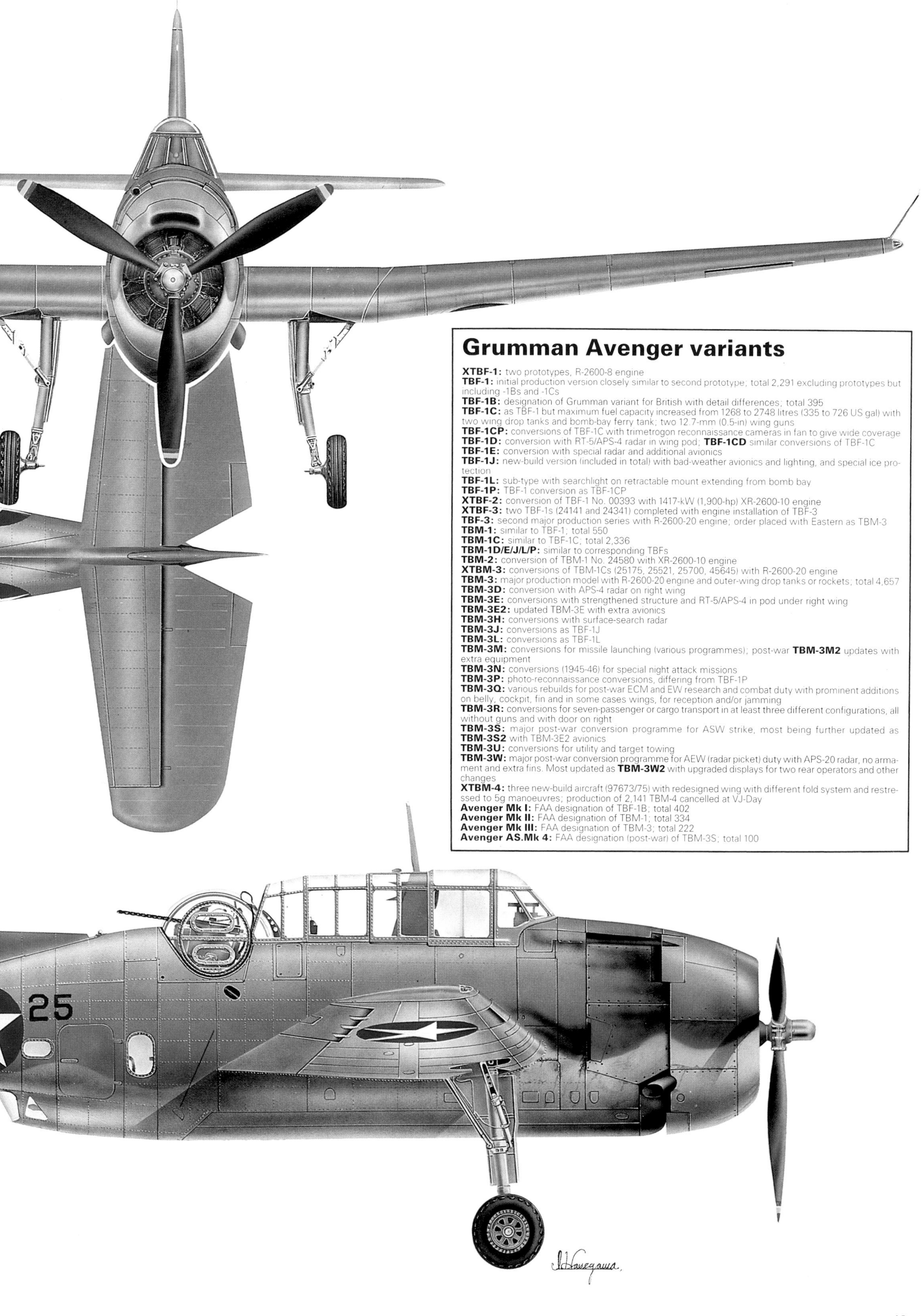

Grumman Avenger variants

XTBF-1: two prototypes, R-2600-8 engine
TBF-1: initial production version closely similar to second prototype; total 2,291 excluding prototypes but including -1Bs and -1Cs
TBF-1B: designation of Grumman variant for British with detail differences; total 395
TBF-1C: as TBF-1 but maximum fuel capacity increased from 1268 to 2748 litres (335 to 726 US gal) with two wing drop tanks and bomb-bay ferry tank; two 12.7-mm (0.5-in) wing guns
TBF-1CP: conversions of TBF-1C with trimetrogon reconnaissance cameras in fan to give wide coverage
TBF-1D: conversion with RT-5/APS-4 radar in wing pod; **TBF-1CD** similar conversions of TBF-1C
TBF-1E: conversion with special radar and additional avionics
TBF-1J: new-build version (included in total) with bad-weather avionics and lighting, and special ice protection
TBF-1L: sub-type with searchlight on retractable mount extending from bomb bay
TBF-1P: TBF-1 conversion as TBF-1CP
XTBF-2: conversion of TBF-1 No. 00393 with 1417-kW (1,900-hp) XR-2600-10 engine
XTBF-3: two TBF-1s (24141 and 24341) completed with engine installation of TBF-3
TBF-3: second major production series with R-2600-20 engine; order placed with Eastern as TBM-3
TBM-1: similar to TBF-1; total 550
TBM-1C: similar to TBF-1C; total 2,336
TBM-1D/E/J/L/P: similar to corresponding TBFs
TBM-2: conversion of TBM-1 No. 24580 with XR-2600-10 engine
XTBM-3: conversions of TBM-1Cs (25175, 25521, 25700, 45645) with R-2600-20 engine
TBM-3: major production model with R-2600-20 engine and outer-wing drop tanks or rockets; total 4,657
TBM-3D: conversion with APS-4 radar on right wing
TBM-3E: conversions with strengthened structure and RT-5/APS-4 in pod under right wing
TBM-3E2: updated TBM-3E with extra avionics
TBM-3H: conversions with surface-search radar
TBM-3J: conversions as TBF-1J
TBM-3L: conversions as TBF-1L
TBM-3M: conversions for missile launching (various programmes); post-war **TBM-3M2** updates with extra equipment
TBM-3N: conversions (1945-46) for special night attack missions
TBM-3P: photo-reconnaissance conversions, differing from TBF-1P
TBM-3Q: various rebuilds for post-war ECM and EW research and combat duty with prominent additions on belly, cockpit, fin and in some cases wings, for reception and/or jamming
TBM-3R: conversions for seven-passenger or cargo transport in at least three different configurations, all without guns and with door on right
TBM-3S: major post-war conversion programme for ASW strike, most being further updated as **TBM-3S2** with TBM-3E2 avionics
TBM-3U: conversions for utility and target towing
TBM-3W: major post-war conversion programme for AEW (radar picket) duty with APS-20 radar, no armament and extra fins. Most updated as **TBM-3W2** with upgraded displays for two rear operators and other changes
XTBM-4: three new-build aircraft (97673/75) with redesigned wing with different fold system and restressed to 5g manoeuvres; production of 2,141 TBM-4 cancelled at VJ-Day
Avenger Mk I: FAA designation of TBF-1B; total 402
Avenger Mk II: FAA designation of TBM-1; total 334
Avenger Mk III: FAA designation of TBM-3; total 222
Avenger AS.Mk 4: FAA designation (post-war) of TBM-3S; total 100

Mitsubishi A6M5c Reisen

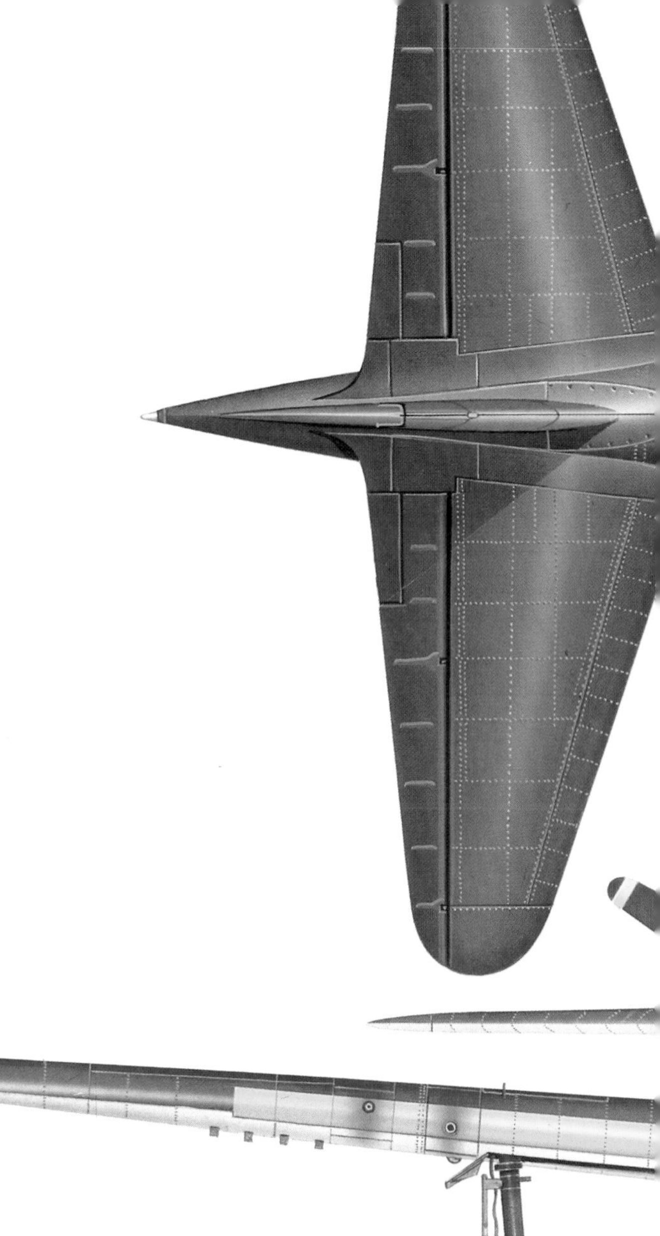

Specification

Mitsubishi A6M5c Reisen
Type: carrier-based fighter-bomber
Powerplant: one 843-kW (1,130-hp) Nakajima NK1F Sakae 21 radial piston engine
Performance: maximum speed 565 km/h (351 mph); cruising speed 370 km/h (230 mph); climb to 6000 m (19,685 ft) in 7 minutes; service ceiling 11740 m (38,520 ft); maximum range 1922 km (1,194 miles)
Weights: empty 1876 kg (4,136 lb); maximum take-off 2733 kg (6,025 lb)
Dimensions: span 11.00 m (36 ft 1 in); length 9.12 m (29 ft 11.25 in); height 3.50 m (11 ft 6 in); wing area 21.3 m^2 (229.27 sq ft)
Armament: one 13.2-mm (0.52-in) Type 3 heavy machine-gun in the fuselage decking (breech in the cockpit), two 20-mm Type 99 cannon in the wings and two 13.2-mm (0.52-in) Type 3 guns in the wings outboard of the cannon, plus two 60-kg (132-lb) bombs under the wings (suicide mission, one 250-kg/551-lb bomb)

Mitsubishi A6M Reisen variants

Mitsubishi A6M1: first two prototypes, powered by the 582-kW (780-hp) Zuisei 13 engine
Mitsubishi A6M2: initial production version, powered by the 701-kW (940-hp) Sakae 12 engine, with an armament of two 20-mm and two 7.7-mm (0.303-in) guns, span 12.00 m (39 ft 4.5 in) and normal take-off weight 2410 kg (5,313 lb); initial aircraft of the batch, up to c/n 21, had an unreinforced rear spar, aircraft from c/n 22 onwards had the reinforced rear spar (both sub-types being designated **Model 11**), and from c/n 65 the wingtips were capable of manual folding (the sub-type being designated **Model 21**)
Mitsubishi A6M3 Model 32: improved production model powered by the 843-kW (1,130-hp) Sakae 21; from the fourth aircraft 20-mm cannon ammunition was increased, and later aircraft had square-tipped wings of 11.00 m (36 ft 1 in) span compared with the **A6M3 Model 22**'s rounded tips of 12.00 m (39 ft 4.5 in); normal take-off weight 2544 kg (5,609 lb)
Mitsubishi A6M4: unsuccessful experimental variant with turbocharged Sakae engine
Mitsubishi A6M5 Model 52: improved A6M3 with thicker wing skins, rounded wingtips and thrust-augmenting exhaust stacks; normal take-off weight 2733 kg (6,025 lb)
Mitsubishi A6M5a Model 52A: derivative of the A6M5 with thicker skins and improved Type 99 Model 2 Mark 3 cannon
Mitsubishi A6M5 Model 52B: improved A6M5a with extra protection, fire extinguishing system for the fuel tanks, and one 7.7-mm (0.303-in) machine-gun replaced by a 13.2-mm (0.52-in) Type 3 weapon
Mitsubishi A6M5c Model 52C: yet further improved model, with two 13.2-mm (0.52-in) Type 3 machine-guns added outboard of the cannon, armour behind the pilot, extra fuel capacity, and racks for eight 10-kg (22-lb) unguided air-to-air rockets
Mitsubishi A6M6c Model 53C: improved A6M5c with 903-kW (1,210-hp) Sakae 31 plus methanol/water boost, and self-sealing wing tanks
Mitsubishi A6M7 Model 63: dive-bomber version of the A6M6c intended for use from small carriers; centreline provision for one 250-kg (551-lb) bomb and underwing points for two 350-litre (77-Imp gal) drop tanks
Mitsubishi A6M8 Model 64: uprated model with 1164-kW (1,560-hp) Kinsei 62 engine, no fuselage guns, better protection, and normal take-off weight 3150 kg (6,945 lb)
Mitsubishi A6M2-K: dual-control trainer version of the A6M2
Mitsubishi A6M5-K: dual-control version of the A6M5
Nakajima A6M2-N: floatplane version of the A6M2 with single main float and two underwing stabilising floats; normal take-off weight 2460 kg (5,423 lb)

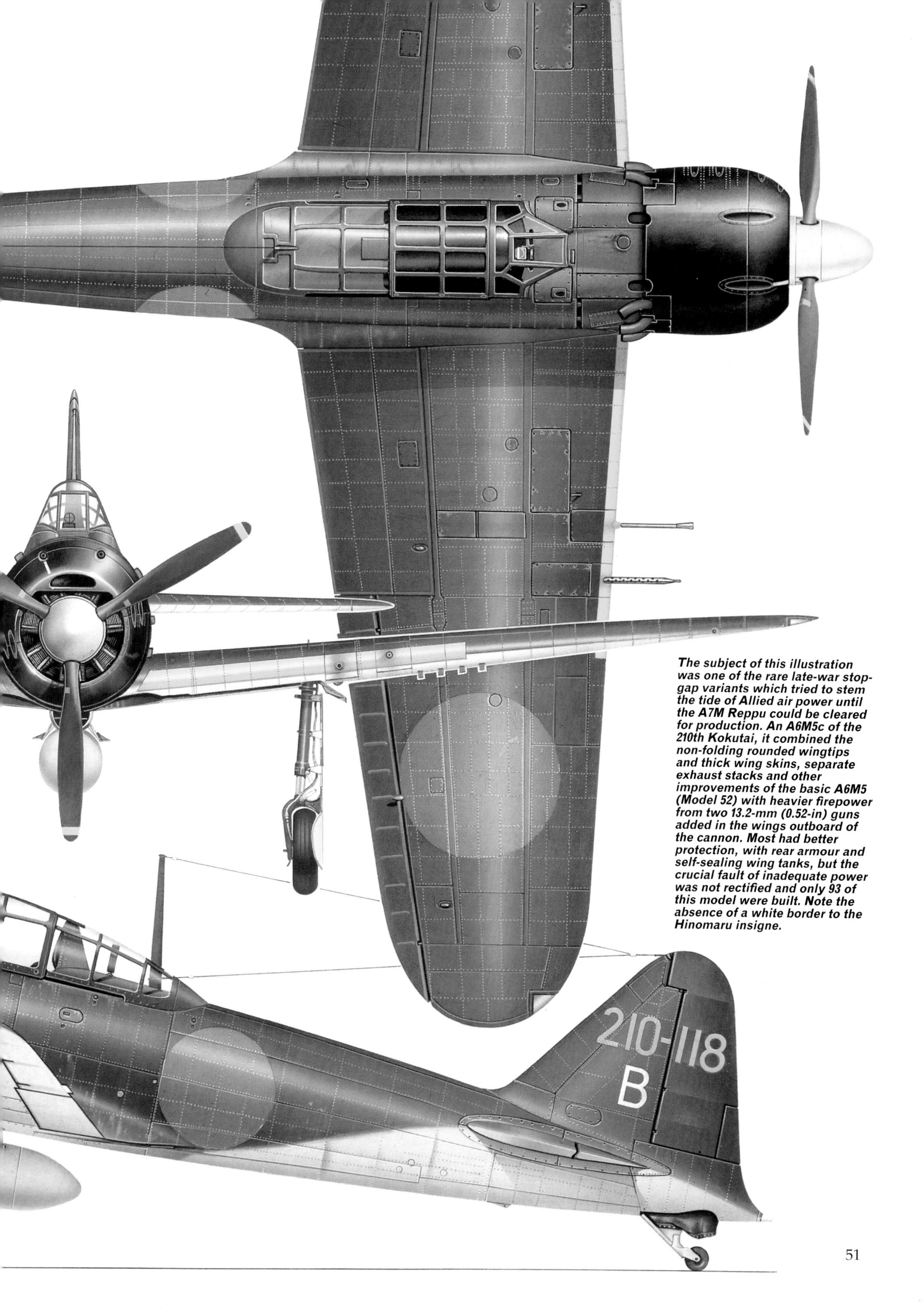

The subject of this illustration was one of the rare late-war stop-gap variants which tried to stem the tide of Allied air power until the A7M Reppu could be cleared for production. An A6M5c of the 210th Kokutai, it combined the non-folding rounded wingtips and thick wing skins, separate exhaust stacks and other improvements of the basic A6M5 (Model 52) with heavier firepower from two 13.2-mm (0.52-in) guns added in the wings outboard of the cannon. Most had better protection, with rear armour and self-sealing wing tanks, but the crucial fault of inadequate power was not rectified and only 93 of this model were built. Note the absence of a white border to the Hinomaru insigne.

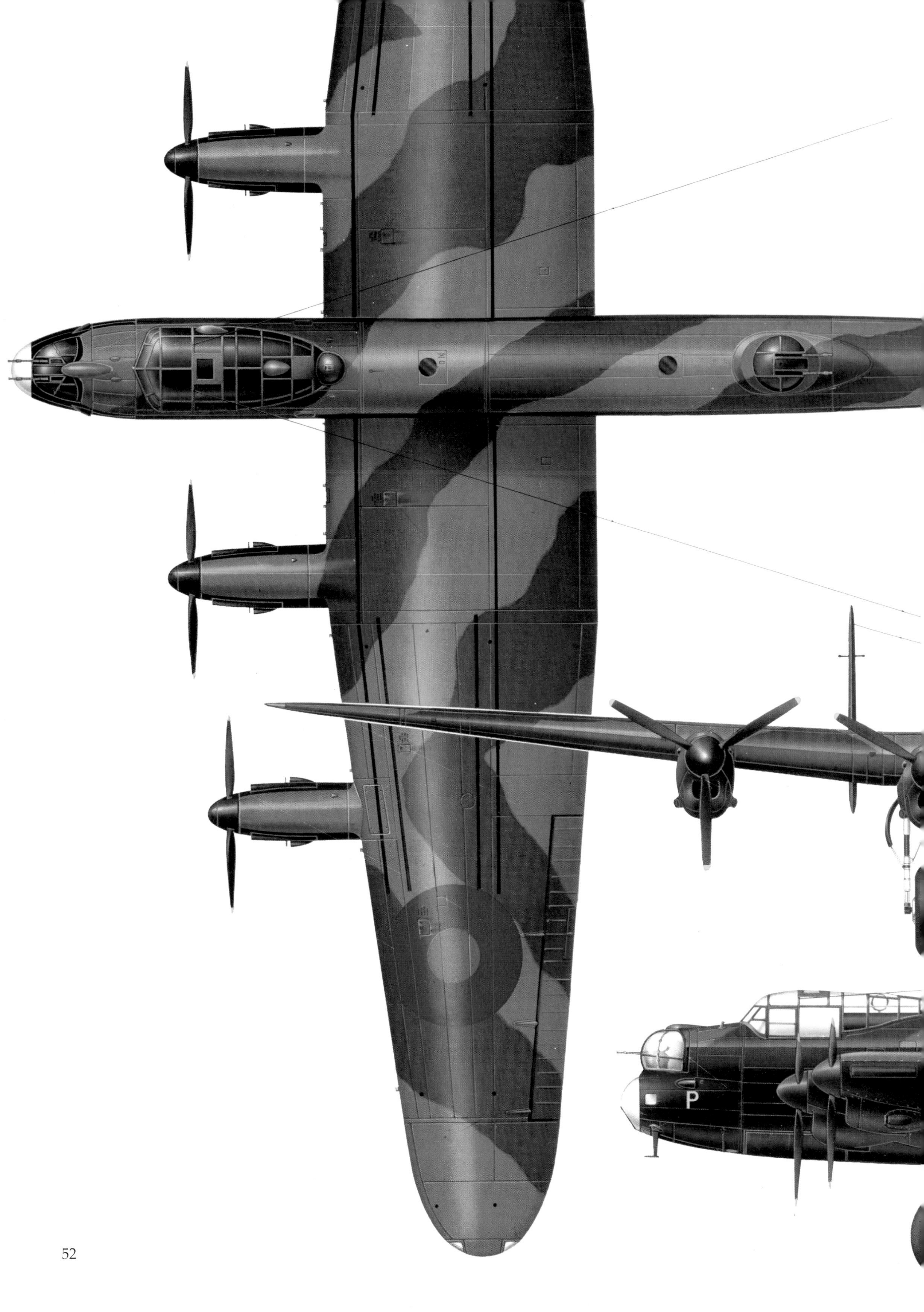
P

Specification
Avro Lancaster I
Type: seven-seat heavy bomber
Powerplant: four 955-kW (1,280-hp) Rolls-Royce Merlin XX, or 1089-kW (1,460-hp) Merlin 22 or 1223-kW (1,640-hp) Merlin 24 inverted inline piston engines
Performance: maximum speed 442 km/h (275 mph) at 4570 m (15,000 ft); cruising speed 322 km/h (200 mph) at 4570 m (15,000 ft); service ceiling 5790 m (19,000 ft); range 4072 km (2,530 miles) with 3175-kg (7,000-lb) payload
Weights: empty 16783 kg (37,000 lb); maximum take-off 30845 kg (68,000 lb)
Dimensions: span 31.09 m (102 ft 0 in); length 21.18 m (69 ft 6 in); height 6.25 m (20 ft 6 in); wing area 120.49 m^2 (1,297 sq ft)
Armament: (early production model) nine 7.7-mm (0.303-in) Browning machine-guns (one in FN.64 ventral, two each in FN.5 nose and FN.50 dorsal, and four in FN.20 tail turrets), plus up to 9979 kg (22,000 lb) of bombs

This Lancaster B.Mk I is typical of the many which served RAF Bomber Command on the nightly offensive against the Reich. Standard camouflage of dark green/dark earth upper surfaces and black undersides was virtually fleet-wide. The 'EM' code denoted No. 207 Squadron, which gained fame in November 1940 as the first Manchester squadron. Lancasters arrived in March 1942, and served with the unit until it re-equipped with Lincolns in August 1949. Thereafter Washingtons, Canberras and Valiants were its equipment, before suffering the ignominy of being resurrected as the Southern Communications Squadron. During its wartime career, the squadron earned seven DSOs, 115 DFCs and 92 DFMs. Its most famous action occurred on 17 October 1942 when, during a low-level attack on le Creusot, one of the squadron's Lancasters shot down two Arado Ar 196 floatplanes and damaged a third while limping along on three engines.

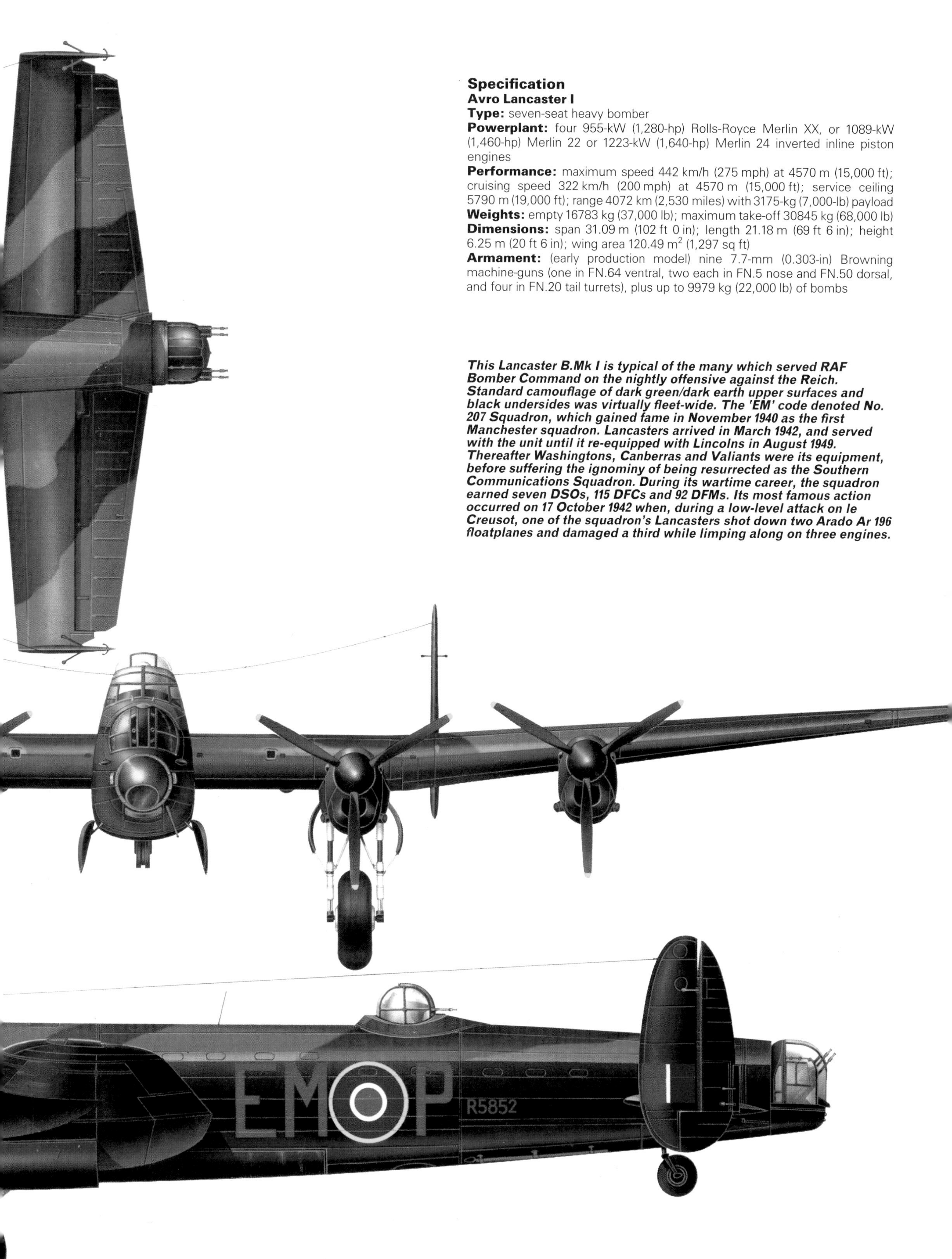

Dewoitine D.520

Factory-fresh production D.520, no. 494, in March 1942 at Toulouse, displaying the mandatory red-and-yellow stripes worn by Vichy aircraft. The photo well illustrates the aft location of the cockpit, providing an excellent downward field of view behind the wing, but demanding considerable weaving during taxiing.

Dewoitine D.520 variants

D.520.01: first prototype; Hispano-Suiza 12Y-21 engine; no armament
D.520.02: second prototype; HS 12Y-29 engine; one cannon and two machine-guns
D.520.03: third prototype; HS 12Y-31 engine and Szydlowski supercharger
D.520: total of 905 production aircraft of which 437 were completed before the fall of France in June 1940, and 468 were produced from August 1941 onwards; the former aircraft had HS 12Y-45 engines driving Ratier propellers and 197 of the latter had HS 12Y-49 engines driving Chauvière propellers; many served with the Luftwaffe, 60 with the Regia Aeronautica, 120 with the Bulgarian air force and some with the Romanian air force
D.520Z: single aircraft (the 465th production D.520) test flown with alternative engine cooling system and Messier landing gear
SE.520Z: projected development of D.520Z with Hispano-Suiza 12Z engine and increased armament; one prototype only
D.521.01: single aircraft (the 41st production D.520) test flown with Rolls-Royce Merlin III engine
D.523: single aircraft (the 45th production D.520) test flown with Hispano-Suiza 12Y-51 engine
D.524: the D.521.01 (see above) re-engined with Hispano-Suiza 12Z-89ter, but reverted to standard D.520
D.550: racing aircraft produced in 1939 with Hispano-Suiza 12Ycrs (later 12Y-51) engine
D.551: military version of the D.550; total of 18 aircraft produced but never flown; HS 12Y-51 engine
HD.780: floatplane version produced experimentally as a D.520 conversion

Specification

Dewoitine D.520
Type: single-seat interceptor fighter
Powerplant: one 634-kW (850-hp) Hispano-Suiza 12Y-45 12-cylinder Vee liquid-cooled piston engine
Performance: maximum speed 535 km/h (332 mph) at 5500 m (18,045 ft); climb to 4000 m (13,125 ft) in 5 minutes 48 seconds; service ceiling 10250 m (33,630 ft); normal range 890 km (553 miles); maximum range 1540 km (957 miles)
Weights: empty 2125 kg (4,685 lb); maximum take-off 2790 kg (6,151 lb)
Dimensions: span 10.2 m (33 ft 5½ in); length 8.76 m (28 ft 8¾ in); height 2.57 m (8 ft 5¼ in); wing area 15.95 m^2 (171.69 sq ft)
Armament: one hub-firing 20-mm Hispano-Suiza HS404 cannon with 60 rounds and four 7.5-mm (0.295-in) MAC 1934 M39 guns in wings with 675 rounds per gun

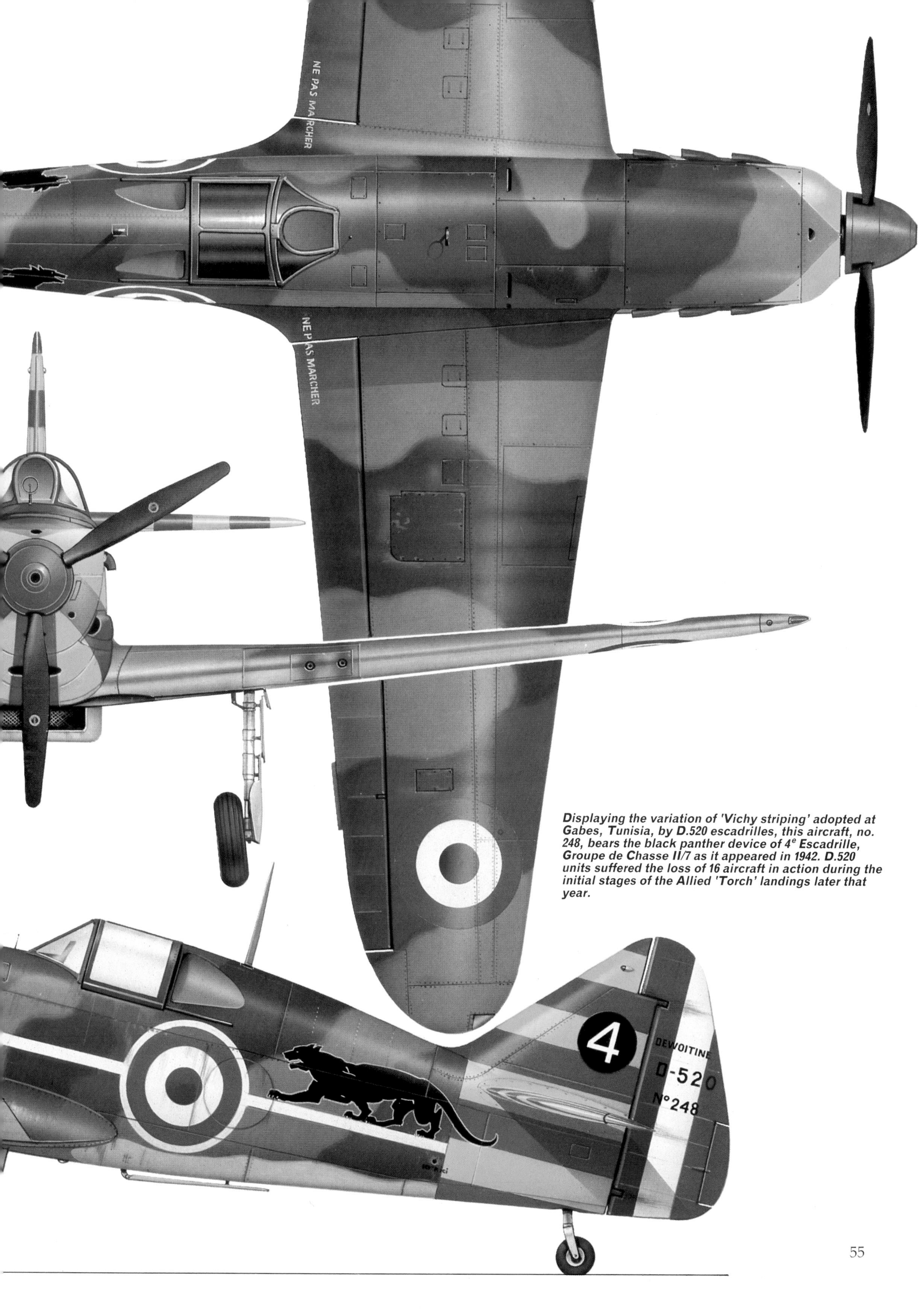

Displaying the variation of 'Vichy striping' adopted at Gabes, Tunisia, by D.520 escadrilles, this aircraft, no. 248, bears the black panther device of 4ᵉ Escadrille, Groupe de Chasse II/7 as it appeared in 1942. D.520 units suffered the loss of 16 aircraft in action during the initial stages of the Allied 'Torch' landings later that year.

Blohm und Voss BV 141B-0

Specification

Blohm und Voss BV 141B-0
Type: army co-operation and tactical reconnaissance platform
Powerplant: one BMW 801A-0 14-cylinder two-row radial engine, rated at 1164 kW (1,560 hp) for take-off
Performance: maximum speed 368 km/h (229 mph) at sea level, 438 km/h (272 mph) at 5000 m (16,400 ft); maximum range 190 km (1,180 miles); normal operational range 1200 km (745 miles); service ceiling 10000 m (32,810 ft)
Weights: empty equipped 4700 kg (10,362 lb); normal loaded 5700 kg (12,566 lb); maximum take-off 6100 kg (13,448 lb)
Dimensions: wing span 17.46 m (57 ft 3¼ in); length 13.95 m (45 ft 9¼ in); height 3.60 m (11 ft 9¾ in); wing area 52.9 m^2 (569.41 sq ft)
Armament: two fixed 7.9-mm (0.31-in) MG 17 machine-guns; one 7.9-mm (0.31-in) MG 15 machine-gun firing aft from flexible mounting; underwing racks for four SC 50 50-kg (110-lb) bombs

This is the fourth BV 141B-0 pre-production aircraft (BV 141 V12), as seen when it was delivered to Tarnewitz for armament trials. During gun-firing tests, it was discovered that the gun ports were too short, meaning the cockpit rapidly filled up with cordite smoke. The B series was considerably different to the A series, with a bigger engine, larger dimensions, equi-taper outboard wing sections and the tailplane offset to port. This last improvement had been introduced to provide the gunner with an almost uninterrupted field of fire from the rear of the cockpit. The gun smoke and other problems haunted the BV 141B programme throughout, and by the time the BV 141 was ready to enter service its role was being adequately filled by the Fw 189.

Iain Wyllie

Hawker Typhoon F.Mk 1B

This aircraft represents the ultimate standard of build of the Typhoon IB, which accounted for all but approximately 105 of the entire production run. The four-bladed propeller was introduced in 1943 but did not completely supplant the original unit. The aircraft shown flew with No. 181 Sqn, 2nd Tactical Air Force, serving in France in June 1944, and is armed with rockets.

Specification

Hawker Typhoon F.Mk 1B (early production)

Type: single-seat fighter-bomber

Powerplant: one 1626-kW (2, 180-hp) Napier Sabre IIA inline piston engine

Performance: maximum speed (clean) 652 km/h (405 mph) at 5485 m (18,000 ft); time to 4570 m (15,000 ft) from sea level, 5 minutes 55 seconds; service ceiling 10670 m (34,000 ft); range (clean) 982 km (610 miles), and with 910-kg (2,000-lb) bombs 821 km (510 miles)

Weights: empty 3992 kg (8,800 lb); maximum take-off 6010 kg (13,250 lb)

Dimensions: span 12.67 m (41 ft 7 in); length 9.73 m (31 ft 11 in); height 4.52 m (14 ft 10 in); wing area 25.9 m^2 (279 sq ft)

Armament: four 20-mm Hispano cannon each with 140 rounds, plus two bombs of up to 454 kg (1,000 lb) each, or eight 27-kg (60-lb) rockets or other stores such as 205-litre (45-Imp gal) drop tanks.

Dornier Do 217N-2/R22

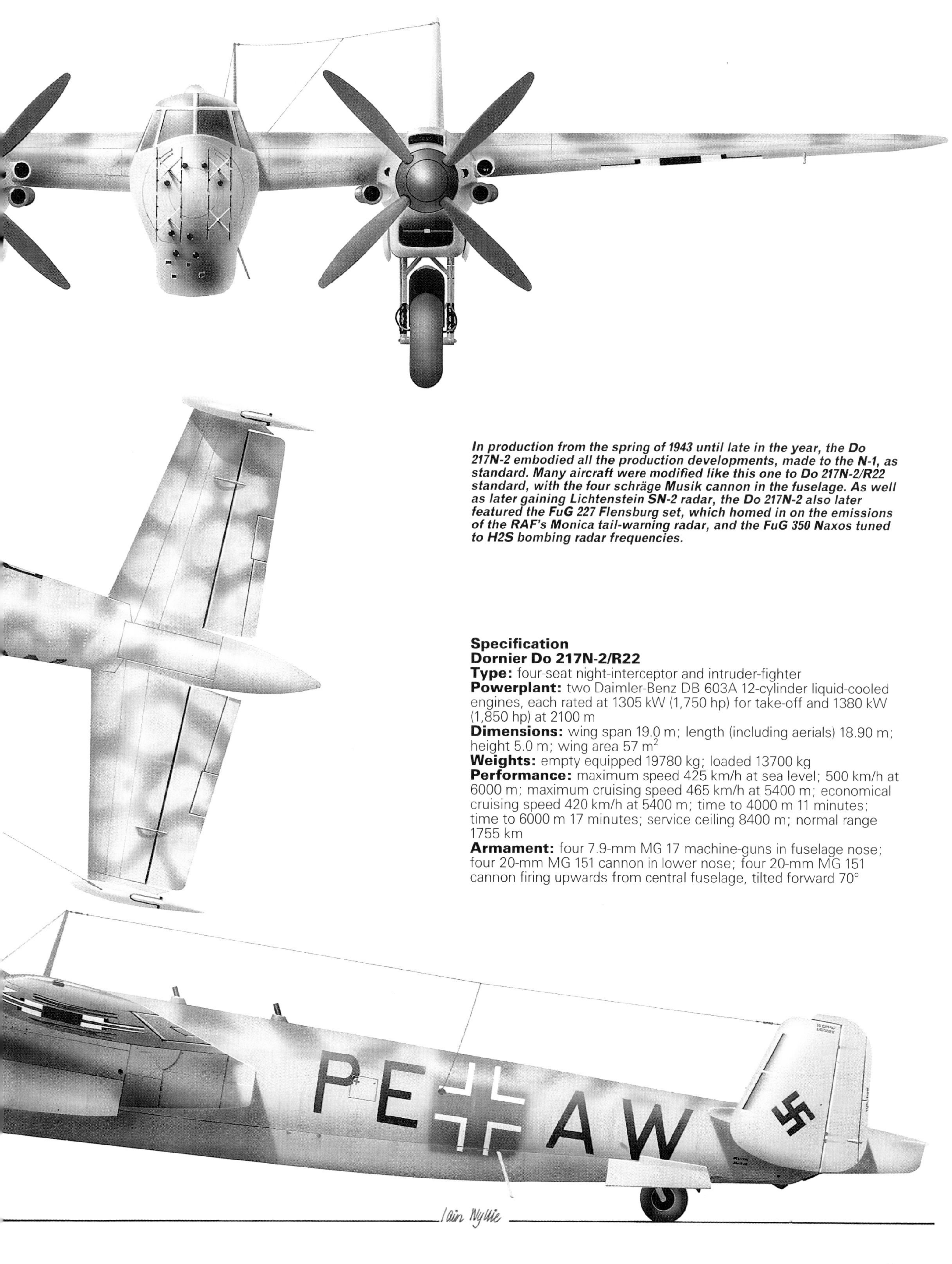

In production from the spring of 1943 until late in the year, the Do 217N-2 embodied all the production developments, made to the N-1, as standard. Many aircraft were modified like this one to Do 217N-2/R22 standard, with the four schräge Musik cannon in the fuselage. As well as later gaining Lichtenstein SN-2 radar, the Do 217N-2 also later featured the FuG 227 Flensburg set, which homed in on the emissions of the RAF's Monica tail-warning radar, and the FuG 350 Naxos tuned to H2S bombing radar frequencies.

Specification
Dornier Do 217N-2/R22
Type: four-seat night-interceptor and intruder-fighter
Powerplant: two Daimler-Benz DB 603A 12-cylinder liquid-cooled engines, each rated at 1305 kW (1,750 hp) for take-off and 1380 kW (1,850 hp) at 2100 m
Dimensions: wing span 19.0 m; length (including aerials) 18.90 m; height 5.0 m; wing area 57 m^2
Weights: empty equipped 19780 kg; loaded 13700 kg
Performance: maximum speed 425 km/h at sea level; 500 km/h at 6000 m; maximum cruising speed 465 km/h at 5400 m; economical cruising speed 420 km/h at 5400 m; time to 4000 m 11 minutes; time to 6000 m 17 minutes; service ceiling 8400 m; normal range 1755 km
Armament: four 7.9-mm MG 17 machine-guns in fuselage nose; four 20-mm MG 151 cannon in lower nose; four 20-mm MG 151 cannon firing upwards from central fuselage, tilted forward 70°

Savoia-Marchetti S.M.79-I

Specification
Savoia-Marchetti S.M.79-I

Type: four/five-crew medium bomber/torpedo-bomber
Powerplant: three 582-kW (780-hp) Alfa Romeo 126 RC.34 9-cylinder air-cooled radial piston engines
Performance: maximum speed 430 km/h (267 mph) at 4000 m (13,125 ft); climb to 4000 m (13,125 ft) in 13 minutes 15 seconds; service ceiling 6500 m (21,325 ft); maximum range at 340 km/h (211 mph) 3300 km (2,050 miles)
Weights: empty 6950 kg (15,322 lb); maximum take-off 10730 kg (23,655 lb)
Dimensions: span 21.20 m (69 ft 6¾ in); length 15.60 m (51 ft 2 in); height 4.60 m (15 ft 1 in); wing area 61.70 m^2 (664.2 sq ft)
Armament: one fixed 12.7-mm (0.5-in) machine-gun firing forward over cabin roof, guns of the same calibre in dorsal position and in rear of ventral position, one 7.7-mm (0.303-in) machine-gun for beam defence, plus a maximum bomb-load of five 250-kg (551-lb) bombs or one 45-cm (17.7-in) naval torpedo

Savoia-Marchetti S.M.79 variants

S.M.79P: commercial prototype (I-MAGO); originally with Piaggio P.IX Stella RC.2, later with Alfa Romeo 125 RC.35, and Alfa Romeo 126 RC.34 engines
S.M.79C: five racing aircraft; 746-kW (1,000-hp) Piaggio P.XI RC.40 engines
S.M.79T: 11 transatlantic aircraft, plus three S.M.79-1 (BISE, I-BRUN and I-MONI) modified to S.M.79T standard; Piaggio P.XI RC.40 engines
S.M.79B: twin-engine variant; prototype with 768-kW (1,030-hp) Fiat A.80 RC.41 radials; four similar aircraft to Iraq in 1938, and three to Brazil with 694-kW (930-hp) Alfa Romeo 128 RC.18 radials
S.M.79B: (Romanian): 24 Italian-built aircraft with 746-kW (1,000-hp) Gnome-Rhône K-14 Mistral Major radials, and 24 Italian-built aircraft with 910-kW (1,220-hp) Junkers 211 Da inline engines
S.M.79-JR: (Romanian): licence-built (by IAR in Bucharest) aircraft with Junkers Jumo 211Da inverted V-12 engines
S.M.79-I: military protoype for Regia Aeronautica; Piaggio P.IX Stella RC.2 radials
S.M.79-I: production version with Alfa Romeo 126 RC.34 radials for Regia Aeronautica and Aerosiluranti; also 45 aircraft to Yugoslavia; some late-series aircraft with 642-kW (860-hp) Alfa Romeo 128 RC.18 radials; in production 1936-40
S.M.79-II: production version (bombers and torpedo-bombers) with 746-kW (1,000-hp) Piaggio P.XI RC.40 radials; in production 1940-43
S.M.79-III: (sometimes designated **S.579**): production version (bombers and torpedo-bombers) with increased armament; most aircraft without ventral gondola; alternative engines were 746-kW (1,000-hp) Fiat A.80 RC.41 or 1007-kW (1,350-hp) Alfa Romeo 135 RC.32 radials

Savoia-Marchetti S.M.79-II of the 205ª Squadriglia, displaying the Sorci Verdi (Green Mice) emblem adopted from the pre-war S.M.79 record-breaking Sparviero flight led by Colonel Attilio Biseo. Although early in the war Italian bombers tended to be deployed and operated in gruppo strength, battle losses during the final stages of the North African campaign resulted in many such units being disbanded. The 205ª Squadriglia was, however, re-formed as an autonomous unit at Milis, Sardinia, on the eve of the invasion of Sicily in July 1943, albeit with only four serviceable Sparvieri.

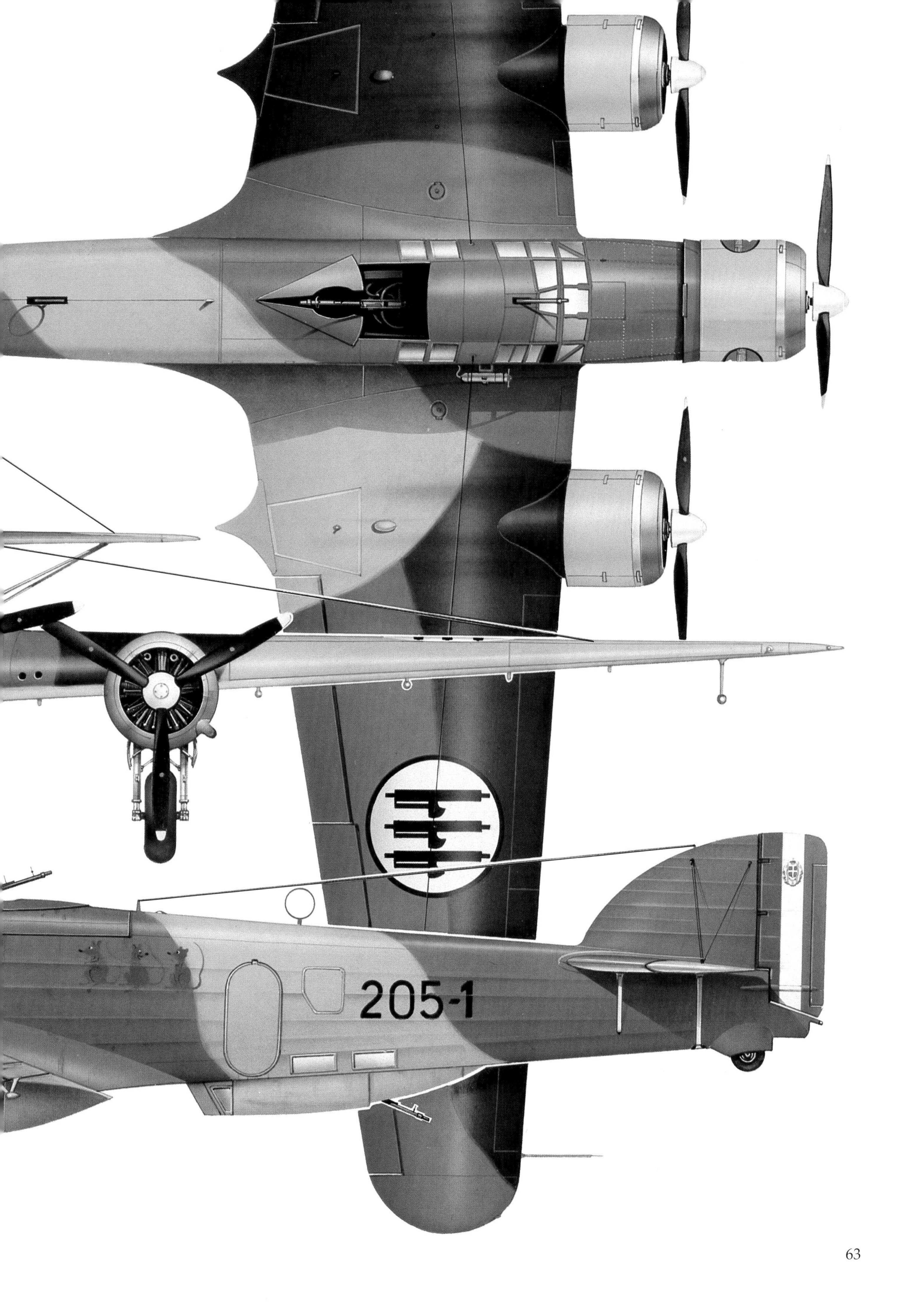
205-1

Macchi MC.202 Series VIII Folgore

Specification
Macchi MC.202 Series VIII Folgore

Type: single-seat fighter
Powerplant: one 802-kW (1,075-hp) Alfa Romeo R.A.1000 RC.41-1 Monsoni (Monsoon) inverted V-12
Performance: maximum speed 600 km/h (373 mph) at 5600 m (18,375 ft); climb to 5000 m (16,405 ft) in 4 minutes 40 seconds; service ceiling 11500 m (37,730 ft); range at maximum take-off weight 765 km (475 miles)
Weights: empty 2490 kg (5,489 lb); maximum take-off 3010 kg (6,636 lb)
Dimensions: span 10.58 m (34 ft 8⅔ in); length 8.85 m (29 ft 0½ in); height 3.50 m (11 ft 5¾ in); wing area 16.82 m^2 (180.83 sq ft)
Armament: two 12.7-mm (0.5-in) Breda-SAFAT machine-guns in nose, each with 360 rounds, and two 7.7-mm (0.303-in) Breda-SAFAT guns in wings, each with 500 rounds

Identified as an aircraft of the 22° Gruppo by the* Spauracchio *(scarecrow) device on the fuselage band, and by the numerals as belonging to the 369ª Squadriglia, this mid-series MC.202 was based at Capodichino, Naples as part of the 53° Stormo CT at the time of the invasion of Sicily in July 1943. Although its maximum speed of 600 km/h (373 mph) was adequate to match Allied fighters of the Spitfire Mk V's generation, the purpose of deploying aircraft such as the MC.202 to defend Italian cities from attacks by Allied bombers was questionable, as their light armament was quite inadequate for the role of bomber-destroyer.

369
2

Douglas A-20G Havoc

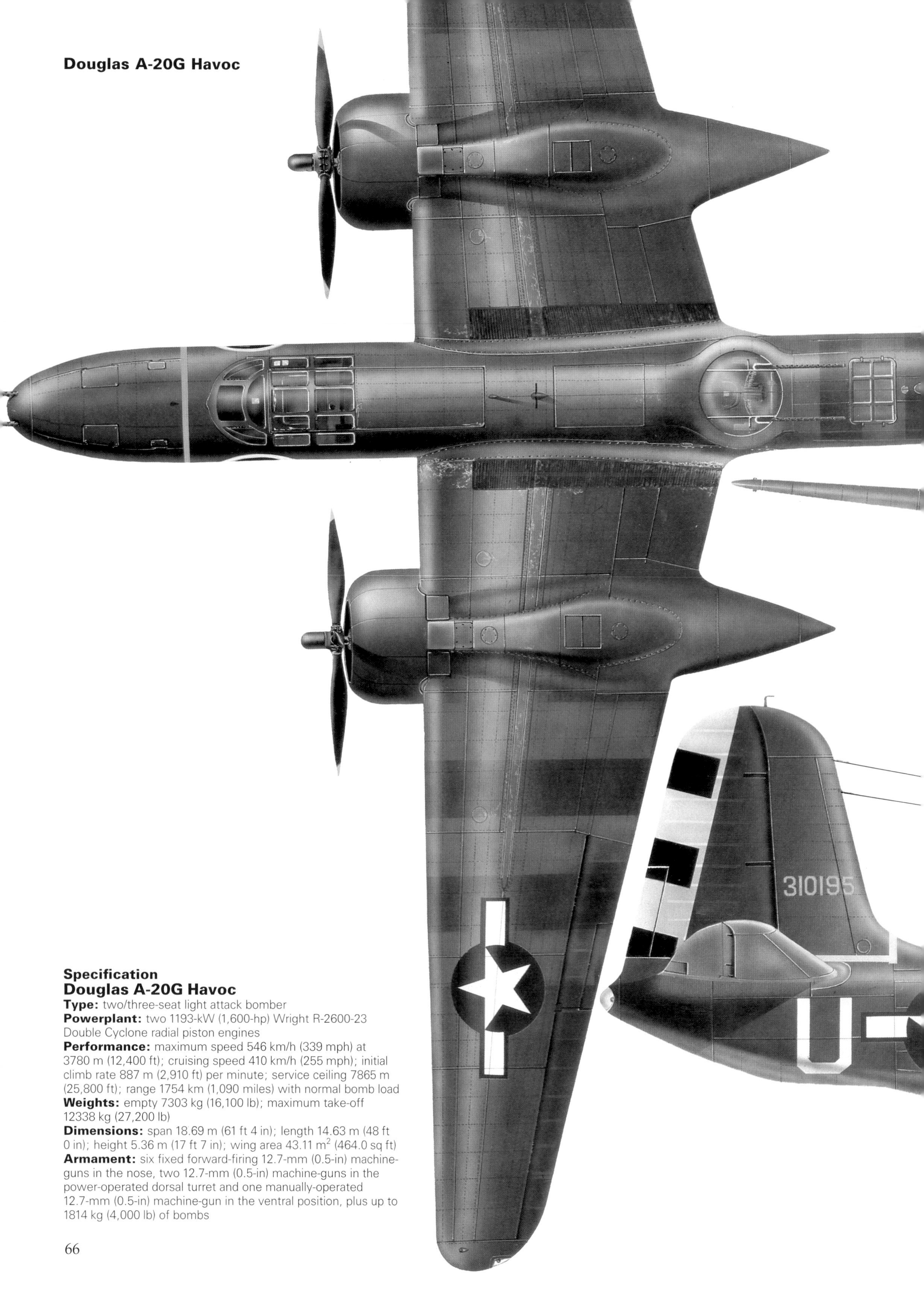

Specification

Douglas A-20G Havoc

Type: two/three-seat light attack bomber
Powerplant: two 1193-kW (1,600-hp) Wright R-2600-23 Double Cyclone radial piston engines
Performance: maximum speed 546 km/h (339 mph) at 3780 m (12,400 ft); cruising speed 410 km/h (255 mph); initial climb rate 887 m (2,910 ft) per minute; service ceiling 7865 m (25,800 ft); range 1754 km (1,090 miles) with normal bomb load
Weights: empty 7303 kg (16,100 lb); maximum take-off 12338 kg (27,200 lb)
Dimensions: span 18.69 m (61 ft 4 in); length 14.63 m (48 ft 0 in); height 5.36 m (17 ft 7 in); wing area 43.11 m^2 (464.0 sq ft)
Armament: six fixed forward-firing 12.7-mm (0.5-in) machine-guns in the nose, two 12.7-mm (0.5-in) machine-guns in the power-operated dorsal turret and one manually-operated 12.7-mm (0.5-in) machine-gun in the ventral position, plus up to 1814 kg (4,000 lb) of bombs

***USAAF** 43-10195 was one of a sub-block of 93 **A**-20**G**-35s built in 1943 at the main **D**ouglas plant at **S**anta Monica. **T**he **A**-20**G**-35 had the rear fuselage 152-mm (6 in) wider behind the **M**artin electric turret, and also had underwing hardpoints which doubled the bomb load from 907 to 1814 kg (2,000 to 4,000 lb). **Q**ueen Julia served with the 646th **B**omb **S**quadron, 410th **B**omb **G**roup, flying intensively from **G**osfield, **E**ssex, **E**ngland, with the **IX B**omber **C**ommand. **O**perations began in early May 1944 against every kind of surface target. **B**y chance, the squadron rudder marking was the same as the 'invasion stripes' applied to all **A**llied aircraft in the theatre on 5 June 1944. **B**y late **S**eptember the **A**llied armies were getting out of range, and the whole group moved to **C**oulommiers, at **T**oulouse, to continue the fight against **G**erman units retreating in southern **F**rance.*

Focke-Wulf Fw 190D-9

A standard Fw 190D-9 of JG 77. Although seen as an interim aircraft to fill in before the definitive Ta 152 could enter service, the Fw 190D was itself an excellent aircraft, blessed with good speed and climb performance. Most German pilots were sceptical of the new variant, but when they had a chance to fly it were most surprised, finding it better than the BMW 801-powered Fw 190A in most respects apart from roll-rate. The Fw 190D-9 put the Luftwaffe fighter units on a par with the later-model Spitfires and Mustangs being flown by the Allies.

Specification

Focke-Wulf Fw 190D-9

Type: single-seat fighter and fighter-bomber

Powerplant: one Junkers Jumo 213A-1 12-cylinder inverted-Vee engine developing 1670 kW (2242 hp) at sea level with MW50 methanol boosting, driving a three-bladed VS 111 constant-speed propeller

Performance: maximum speed 686 km/h (426 mph) at 6600 m (21,654 ft), 575 km/h (357 mph) at sea level; maximum range on internal fuel 837 km (520 miles); climb to 2000 m (6560 ft) 2.1 minutes; climb to 10000 m (32,800 ft) 7.1 minutes

Weights: empty 3490 kg (7,694 lb); normal loaded 4300 kg (9,480 lb); maximum loaded 4840 kg (10670 lb)

Dimensions: wing span 10.5 m (34.4 ft); length 10.19 m (33.4 ft); height 3.36 m (11 ft); wing area 18.3 m^2 (197 sq ft)

Armament: two 20-mm MG 151 cannon with 250 rounds per gun, two 13-mm MG 131 machine-guns with 475 rounds per gun, ETC 504 fuselage rack for one 500-kg SC 500 bomb

Nakajima Ki-43-II-Otsu

Specification

Nakajima Ki-43-II-Otsu
Type: single-seat fighter and fighter-bomber
Powerplant: one 858-kW (1,150-hp) Nakajima Ha-115 14-cylinder air-cooled radial piston engine
Performance: maximum speed 530 km/h (329 mph) at 4000 m (13,125 ft); climb to 5000 m (16,405 ft) in 5 minutes 49 seconds; service ceiling 11200 m (36,750 ft); normal range 1760 km (1,095 miles)
Weights: empty 1910 kg (4,211 lb); maximum take-off 2925 kg (6,450 lb)
Dimensions: span 10.84 m (35 ft 6¾ in); length 8.92 m (29 ft 3$\frac{5}{16}$ in); height 3.27 m (10 ft 8¾ in); wing area 21.4 m^2 (230.4 sq ft)
Armament: two 12.7-mm (0.5-in) Type 1 (Ho-103) machine-guns in the upper fuselage decking, plus two 30-kg (66-lb) or 250-kg (551-lb) bombs

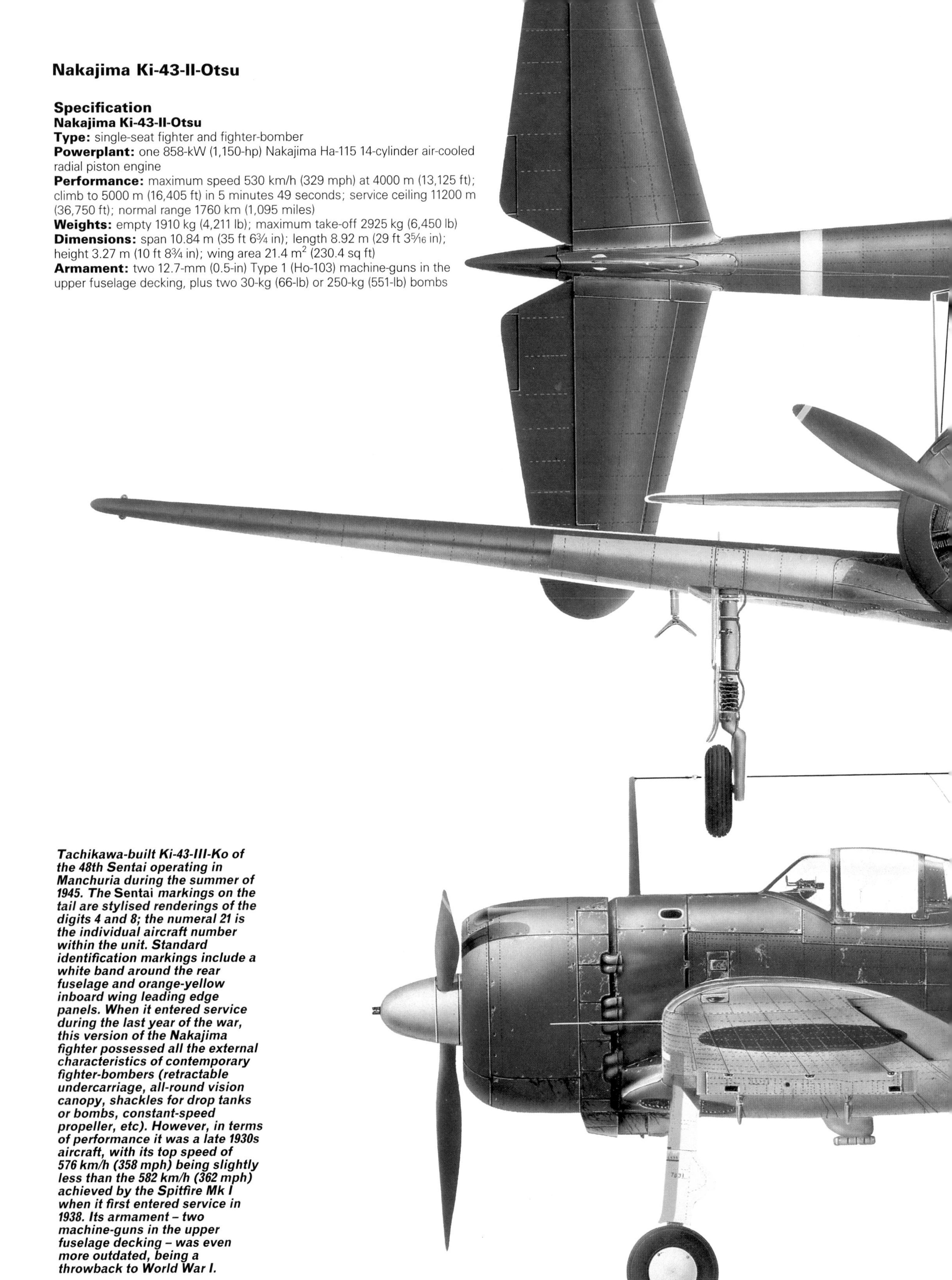

Tachikawa-built Ki-43-III-Ko of the 48th Sentai operating in Manchuria during the summer of 1945. The Sentai markings on the tail are stylised renderings of the digits 4 and 8; the numeral 21 is the individual aircraft number within the unit. Standard identification markings include a white band around the rear fuselage and orange-yellow inboard wing leading edge panels. When it entered service during the last year of the war, this version of the Nakajima fighter possessed all the external characteristics of contemporary fighter-bombers (retractable undercarriage, all-round vision canopy, shackles for drop tanks or bombs, constant-speed propeller, etc). However, in terms of performance it was a late 1930s aircraft, with its top speed of 576 km/h (358 mph) being slightly less than the 582 km/h (362 mph) achieved by the Spitfire Mk I when it first entered service in 1938. Its armament – two machine-guns in the upper fuselage decking – was even more outdated, being a throwback to World War I.

21

North American B-25H Mitchell

Among the most colourfully decorated aircraft of the war were the B-25s that served in the Pacific theatre. Commanded by Colonel Glenn A. Doolittle, the 345th Bomb Group (Medium) moved to Leyte in the Philippines in November 1944, its B-25Js marked with the Group's 'Air Apache' badge prominently on their tails. Among its component squadrons were the 498th 'Falcons' and the 499th 'Bats Outa Hell', the latter displaying enormous bat wings enveloping the aircraft's noses, as typified by this 18-gun B-25J **Betty's Dream.**

Variants

NA-40 (later **NA-40B** and **NA-42**); private-venture prototype; Pratt & Whitney R-1830-56 radials, later Wright GR-2600-A71s
B-25 (NA-62): 24 aircraft (40-2165 to 40-2188); first nine with straight wing dihedral, remainder with gull wing; Wright R-2600-9 radials
B-25A (NA-62A): 40 aircraft (40-2189 to 40-2228); self-sealing tanks and pilot armour; to 17th Bomb Group; Wright R-2600-9 radials
B-25B (NA-62B): 120 aircraft (40-2229 to 40-2242 and 40-2244 to 40-2248; 40-2243 crashed before delivery). 23 to RAF as **Mitchell Mk 1;** some to USSR
B-25C (NA-82): 1,619 aircraft built at Inglewood (42-32233 to 42-32280; 42-32282 to 42-32283; 42-32389 to 42-32532; 42-53332 to 42-53493; 42-64502 to 42-64901); 856 to USAAF; 555 purchased by the UK as **Mitchell Mk II** but 45 retained in Canada; 25 to Brazil; 182 to USSR (including eight lost in transit); some to China and Netherlands Indies Air Corps (two of these later to RAF); R-2600-13 radials
B-25D (NA-82A): 2,290 aircraft built at Dallas (41-29648 to 41-30847; 42-87113 to 42-87612; 43-3280 to 43-3869); all purchased for USAAF but 40 B-25D-15s passed to RAF; 29 delivered to Canada; 688 to USSR; some to Indonesia post-war
XB-25E: one aircraft (42-32281) with hot-air de-icing of wing leading edge
XB-25F: one converted B-25C with electric de-icing of wing leading edge
XB-25G: one prototype (42-32284) with standard US Army 75-mm field gun in nose
B-25G (NA-96): 405 aircraft (42-64902 to 42-65201 plus others); production version with M4 75-mm gun in nose
B-25H (NA-98): 1,000 aircraft (43-4105 to 43-5104); production version with T-13E1 75-mm gun in nose and up to 14 12.7-mm (0.5-in) machine-guns; Wright R-2600-13 radials
B-25J (NA-108): 4,390 aircraft (43-3870 to 43-4104; 43-27473 to 43-28222; 43-35946 to 43-36245; 44-28711 to 44-31510; 44-86692 to 44-86897; 45-8801 to 45-8899); almost all built at Kansas; all purchased for USAAF but 295 passed to RAF as **Mitchell Mk III** (of which 20 were returned to USAAF); deliveries to other air forces included Australia, Bolivia, Brazil (46), Chile, Colombia (3), Cuba, France, Indonesia, Mexico, Peru (20), Uruguay and Venezuela. Wright R-2600-92 radials; 12 12.7-mm (0.5-in) machine-guns
PBJ-1: 706 aircraft (similar to B-25J) for US Navy and US Marine Corps; comprised 50 **PBJ-1C**, 152 **PBJ-1D**, one **PBJ-1G**, 248 **PBJ-1H**, and 255 **PBJ-1J**
F-10: 10 conversions as reconnaissance aircraft from B-24D with nose and rear fuselage cameras
AT-24L 60 advanced trainers converted as **AT-24A, AT-24B, AT-24C** and **AT-24D** from B-25D, B-25G, B-25C and B-25J respectively (later redesignated **TB-25D, TB-25G, TB-25C** and **TB-25J** respectively); 117 **TB-25K** trainers converted from B-25J by Hughes with E-1 radar; 40 **TB-25M** converted with E-5 radar; 90 **TB-25L** and 47 **TB-29N** pilot trainers converted by Hayes
ZB-25C, ZB-25D, ZB-25E, CB-25J and **VB-25J:** conversions of bombers to utility and staff transports post-war

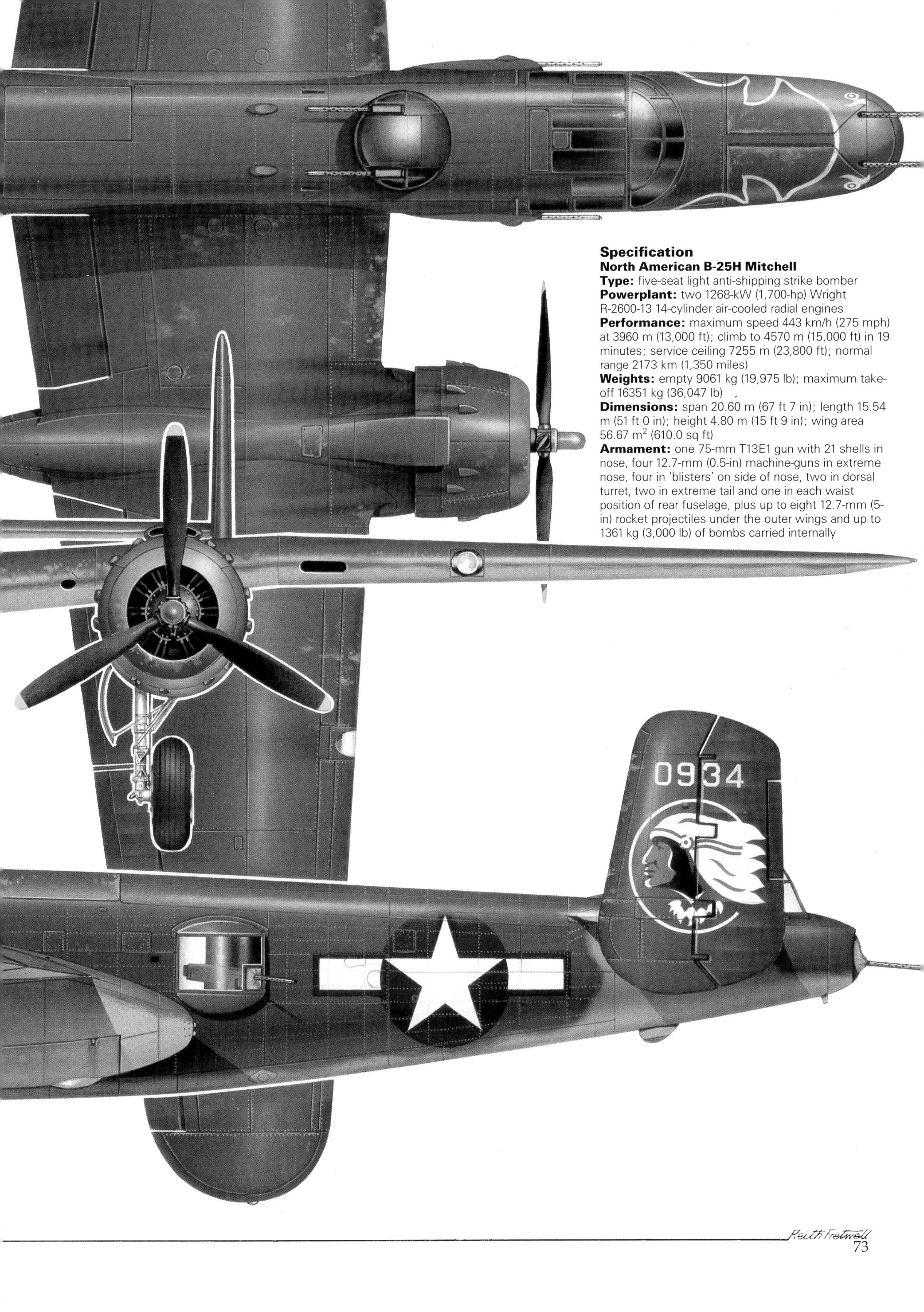

Specification
North American B-25H Mitchell
Type: five-seat light anti-shipping strike bomber
Powerplant: two 1268-kW (1,700-hp) Wright R-2600-13 14-cylinder air-cooled radial engines
Performance: maximum speed 443 km/h (275 mph) at 3960 m (13,000 ft); climb to 4570 m (15,000 ft) in 19 minutes; service ceiling 7255 m (23,800 ft); normal range 2173 km (1,350 miles)
Weights: empty 9061 kg (19,975 lb); maximum take-off 16351 kg (36,047 lb) .
Dimensions: span 20.60 m (67 ft 7 in); length 15.54 m (51 ft 0 in); height 4.80 m (15 ft 9 in); wing area 56.67 m^2 (610.0 sq ft)
Armament: one 75-mm T13E1 gun with 21 shells in nose, four 12.7-mm (0.5-in) machine-guns in extreme nose, four in 'blisters' on side of nose, two in dorsal turret, two in extreme tail and one in each waist position of rear fuselage, plus up to eight 12.7-mm (5-in) rocket projectiles under the outer wings and up to 1361 kg (3,000 lb) of bombs carried internally

Douglas C-47 Skytrain

Specification

Douglas C-47 Skytrain
Type: cargo, supply or 28-seat troop transport, 14-litter ambulance, or glider tug
Powerplant: two 895-kW (1,200-hp) Pratt & Whitney R-1830-92 radial piston engines
Performance: maximum speed 365 km/h (227 mph) at 2285 m (7,500 ft); initial climb rate 287 m (940 ft) per minute; service ceiling 7315 m (24,000 ft); range 2575 km (1,600 miles)
Weights: empty 8256 kg (18,200 lb); maximum take-off 11794 kg (26,000 lb)
Dimensions: span 29.11 m (95 ft 6 in); length 19.43 m (63 ft 9 in); height 5.18 m (17 ft 0 in); wing area 91.69 m^2 (987 sq ft)
Payload: 3629 kg (8,000 lb) to 4536 kg (10,000 lb) of military cargo (depending on aircraft variant)

General Eisenhower is on record as having stated that the C-47 was one of the four principal instruments of Allied victory in World War II (the others being the bazooka, Jeep and atom bomb). A typical example of the Skytrain was this C-47A-65-DL of the 81st Troop Carrier Squadron, 436th Troop Carrier Group, based at Membury in England between 3 March 1944 and February 1945 (it also took part in the airborne assault on Southern France, based at Voltone, Italy, during July and August 1944). The mission tally on 'Buzz Buggy', together with invasion stripes, suggests participation in the Normandy, Southern France, Nijmegen and Bastogne operations, both as a paratrooper and glider tug.

N
2100558

Junkers Ju 87G-1

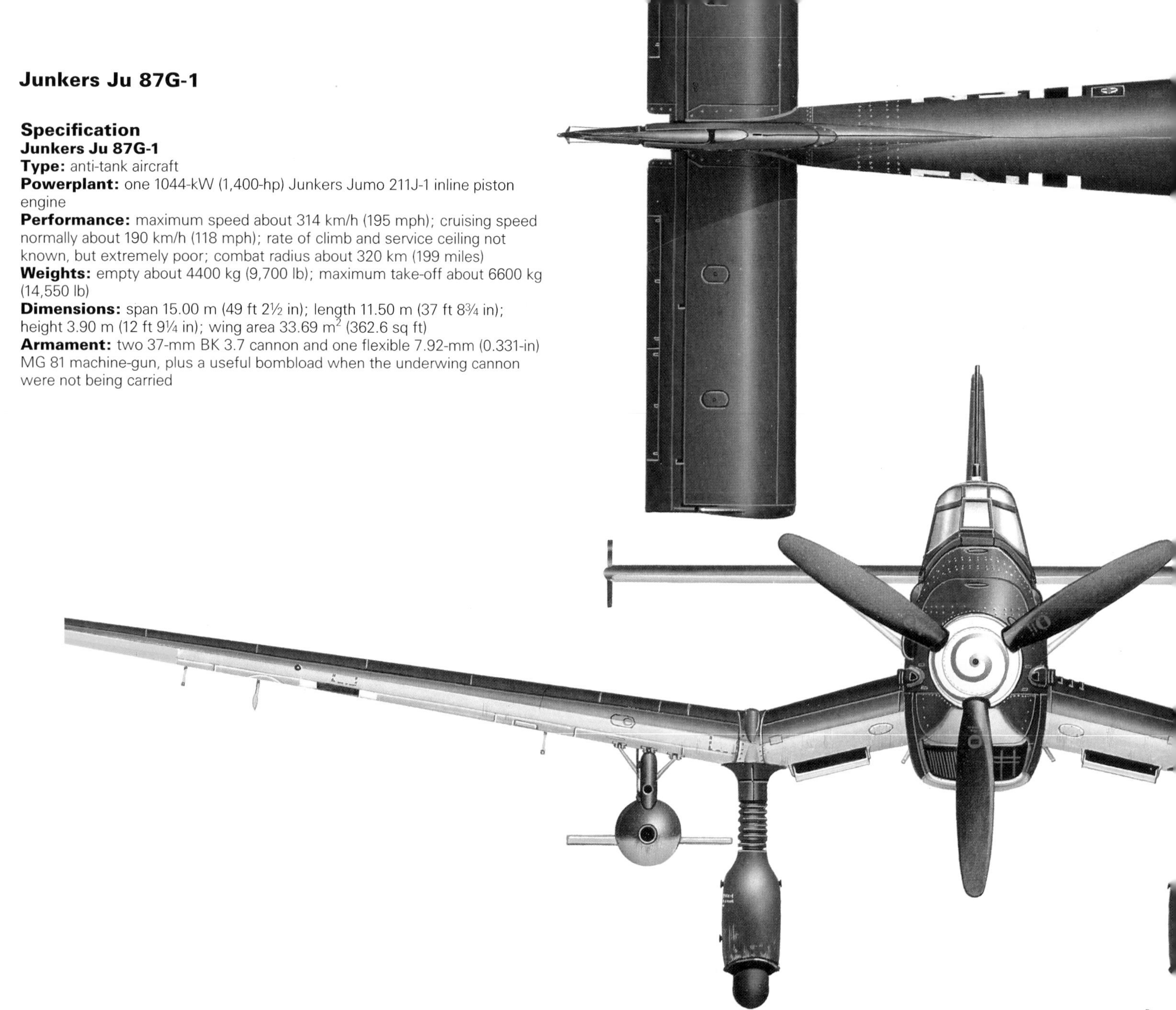

Specification

Junkers Ju 87G-1
Type: anti-tank aircraft
Powerplant: one 1044-kW (1,400-hp) Junkers Jumo 211J-1 inline piston engine
Performance: maximum speed about 314 km/h (195 mph); cruising speed normally about 190 km/h (118 mph); rate of climb and service ceiling not known, but extremely poor; combat radius about 320 km (199 miles)
Weights: empty about 4400 kg (9,700 lb); maximum take-off about 6600 kg (14,550 lb)
Dimensions: span 15.00 m (49 ft 2½ in); length 11.50 m (37 ft 8¾ in); height 3.90 m (12 ft 9¼ in); wing area 33.69 m^2 (362.6 sq ft)
Armament: two 37-mm BK 3.7 cannon and one flexible 7.92-mm (0.331-in) MG 81 machine-gun, plus a useful bombload when the underwing cannon were not being carried

Variants

Junkers Ju 87 V1: first prototype, with 477-kW (640-hp) Rolls-Royce Kestrel
Junkers Ju 87 V2: second prototype 455-kW (610-hp) Jumo 210Aa, hurriedly fitted single-fin tail unit
Junkers Ju 87 V3: third prototype, properly designed tail, engine lowered to improve pilot view
Junkers Ju 87A: first production series, 477-kW (640-hp) Jumo 210Ca or (A-2) 507-kW (680-hp) Jumo 210Da about 200 built (1937-8)
Junkers Ju 87B: 895-kW (1,200-hp) Jumo 211Da, redesigned canopy and fuselage, larger vertical tail, spatted instead of trousered landing gears, bombloads up to 1000 kg (2,205 lb) (total deliveries in various sub-types about 1,300)
Junkers Ju 87C: navalised version intended for use from aircraft-carrier, folding wings, hook, catapult hooks, jettisonable landing gear, flotation gear and extra tankage; operated from land bases
Junkers Ju 87D: major production version, 1044-kW (1,400-hp) Jumo 211J-1 or 1119-kW (1,500-hp) Jumo 211P-1, redesigned airframe with lower drag, bombload up to 1800 kg (3,968-lb), D-2 glider tug, D-3 increased armour, D-4 for torpedo-carrying, D-5 with extended wingtips, D-7 twin MG 151 cannon and night equipment, D-8 as D-7 without night equipment
Junkers Ju 87G-1: conversion of D-3 to attack armoured vehicles with two 37-mm BK 3.7 (Flak 18) guns
Junkers Ju 87H: dual-control trainers without armament, kinked rear canopy with side blisters
Junkers Ju 87R: derivative of Ju 87B-2 with augmented tankage and provision for drop tanks to increase range, normally with single SC250 (551-lb) bomb

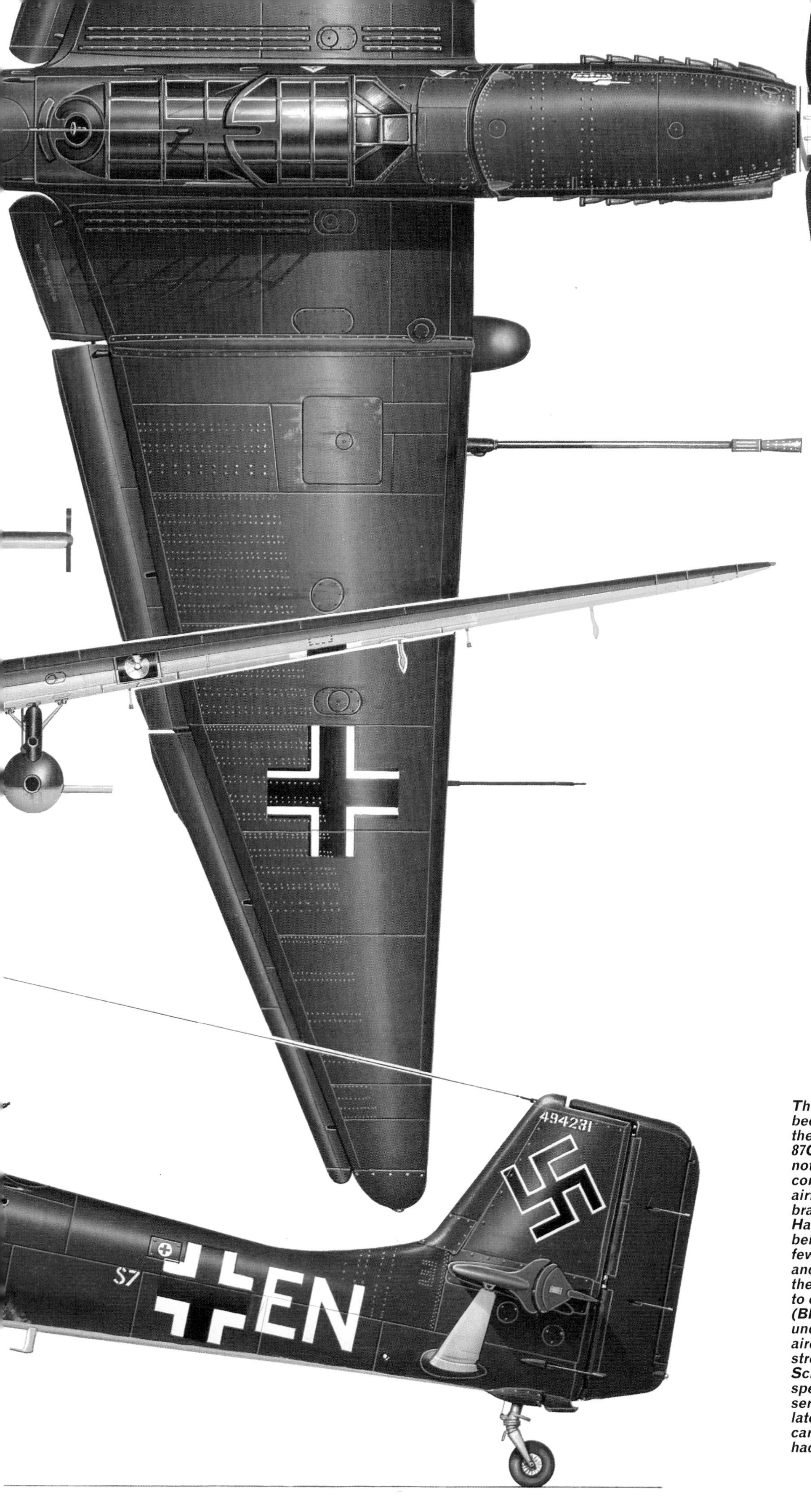

The last variant of the Ju 87 to become operational, apart from the Ju 87H trainer, was the Ju 87G-1 anti-tank model. This was not built as such, but rather converted from Ju 87D-5 airframes. The concept was the brainchild of the extraordinary Hans-Ulrich Rudel, who despite being shot down 30 times flew no fewer than 2,530 combat sorties and destroyed 519 Russian tanks: the basic Ju 87D-5 was adapted to carry a pair of massive Flak 18 (BK 3,7) 37-mm cannon pods under its outer wing panels. The aircraft illustrated was on the strength of II/ Schlachtgeschwader 3, more specifically the unit's 5. Staffel, serving on the Eastern Front in late 1944. The Ju 87G-1 could carry bombs instead of guns, but had no dive-brakes.

Boeing B-29 Superfortress

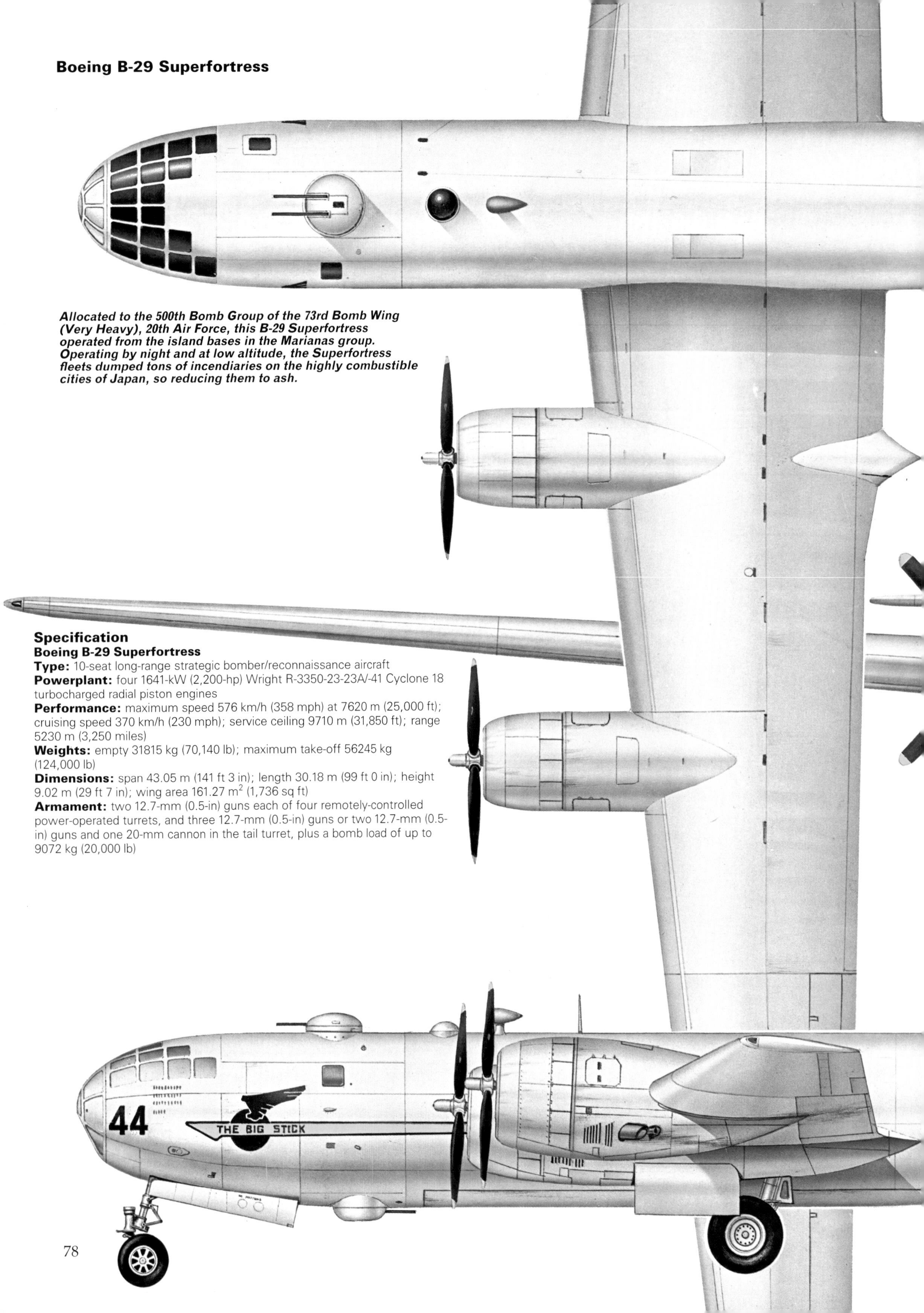

Allocated to the 500th Bomb Group of the 73rd Bomb Wing (Very Heavy), 20th Air Force, this B-29 Superfortress operated from the island bases in the Marianas group. Operating by night and at low altitude, the Superfortress fleets dumped tons of incendiaries on the highly combustible cities of Japan, so reducing them to ash.

Specification

Boeing B-29 Superfortress

Type: 10-seat long-range strategic bomber/reconnaissance aircraft

Powerplant: four 1641-kW (2,200-hp) Wright R-3350-23-23A/-41 Cyclone 18 turbocharged radial piston engines

Performance: maximum speed 576 km/h (358 mph) at 7620 m (25,000 ft); cruising speed 370 km/h (230 mph); service ceiling 9710 m (31,850 ft); range 5230 m (3,250 miles)

Weights: empty 31815 kg (70,140 lb); maximum take-off 56245 kg (124,000 lb)

Dimensions: span 43.05 m (141 ft 3 in); length 30.18 m (99 ft 0 in); height 9.02 m (29 ft 7 in); wing area 161.27 m^2 (1,736 sq ft)

Armament: two 12.7-mm (0.5-in) guns each of four remotely-controlled power-operated turrets, and three 12.7-mm (0.5-in) guns or two 12.7-mm (0.5-in) guns and one 20-mm cannon in the tail turret, plus a bomb load of up to 9072 kg (20,000 lb)

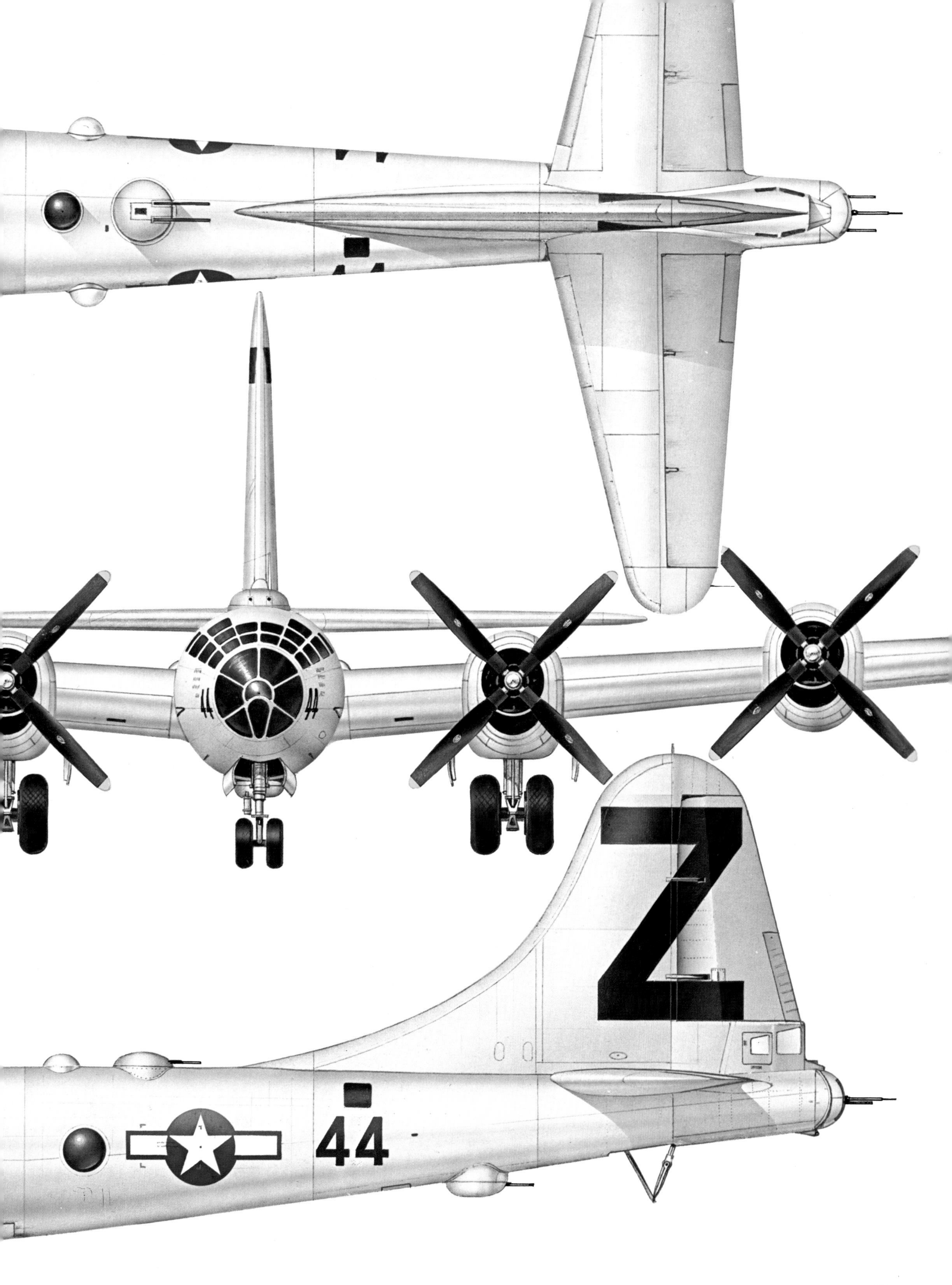
Z
44

Junkers Ju 88G-1

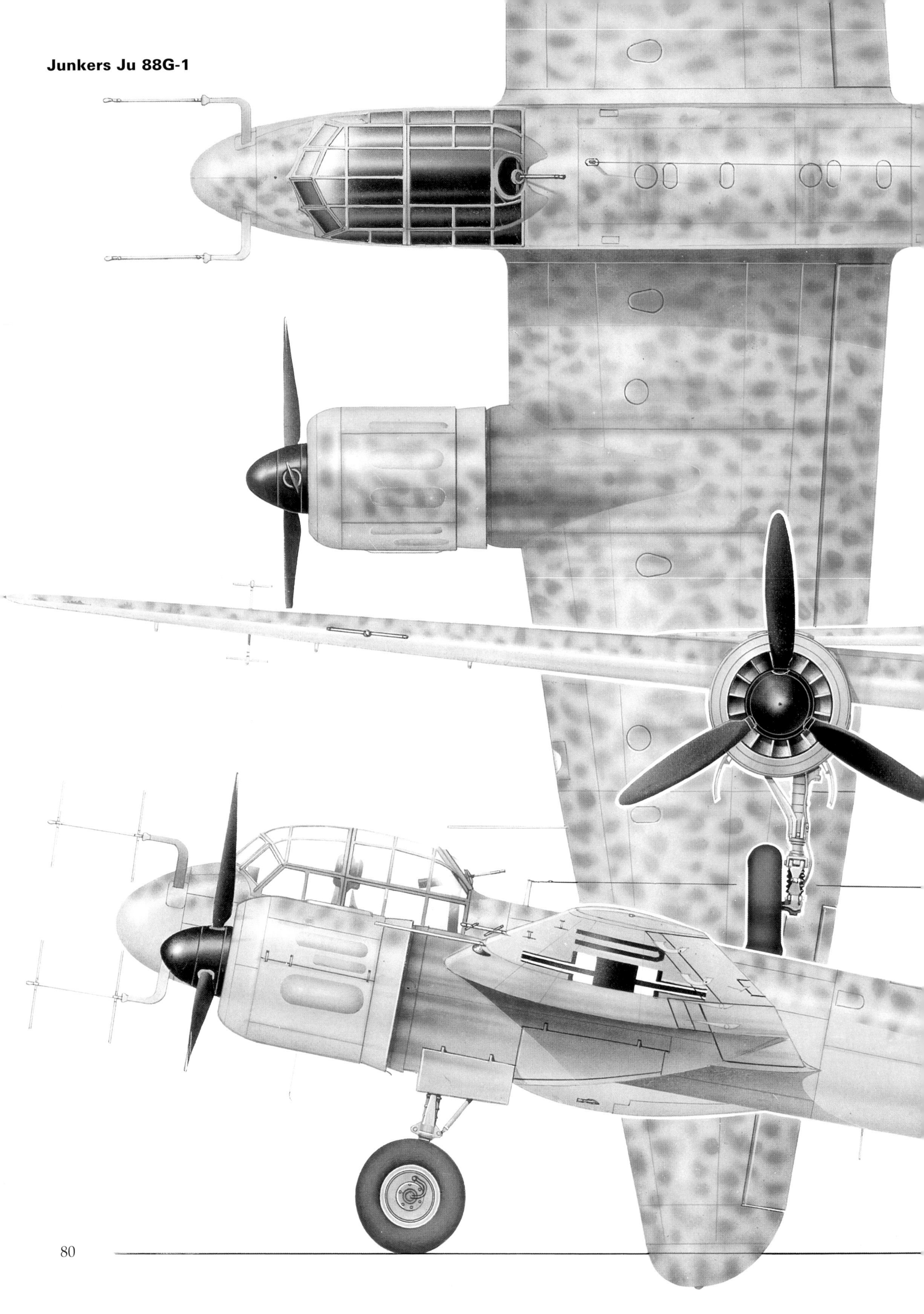

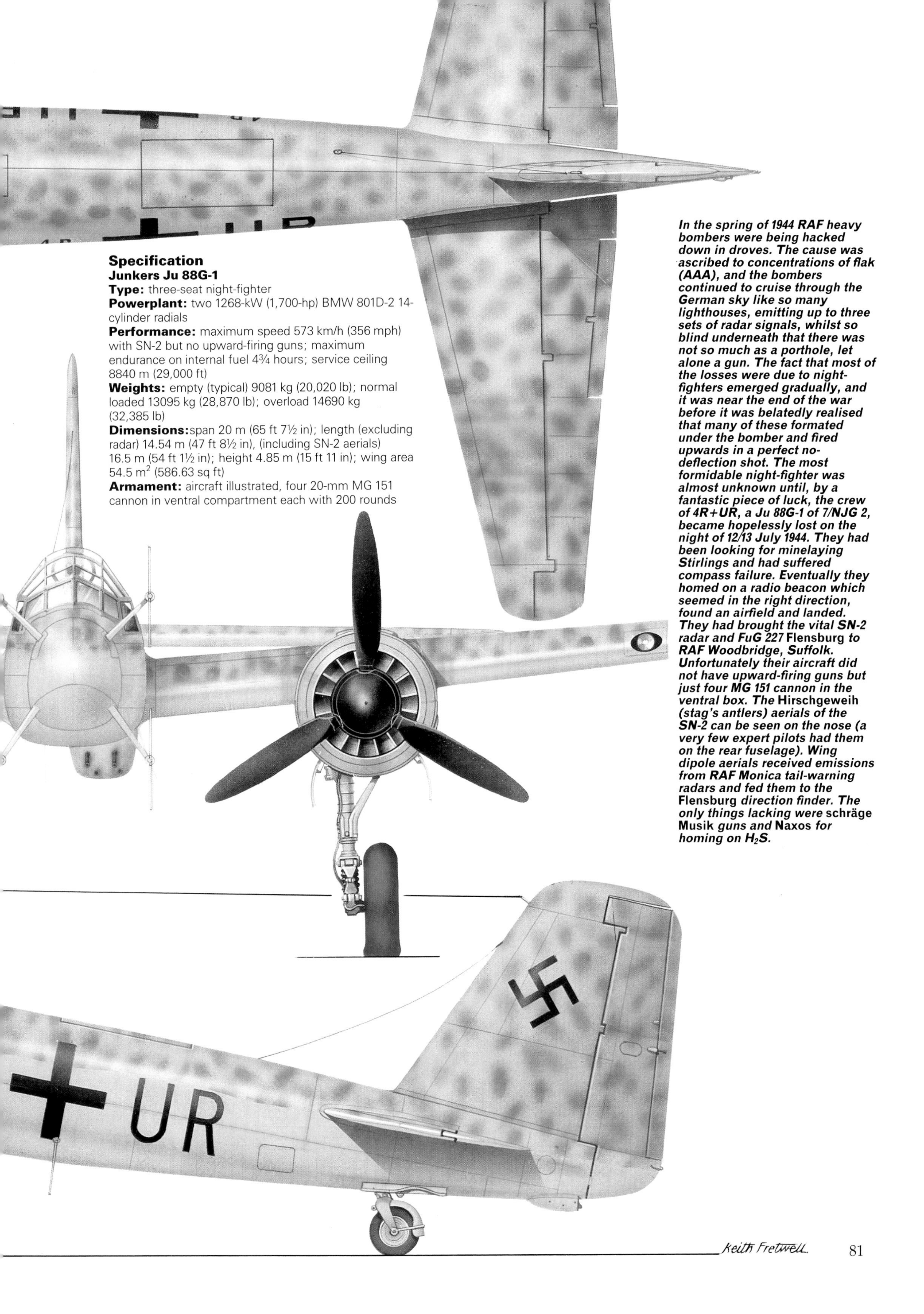

Specification
Junkers Ju 88G-1
Type: three-seat night-fighter
Powerplant: two 1268-kW (1,700-hp) BMW 801D-2 14-cylinder radials
Performance: maximum speed 573 km/h (356 mph) with SN-2 but no upward-firing guns; maximum endurance on internal fuel 4¾ hours; service ceiling 8840 m (29,000 ft)
Weights: empty (typical) 9081 kg (20,020 lb); normal loaded 13095 kg (28,870 lb); overload 14690 kg (32,385 lb)
Dimensions: span 20 m (65 ft 7½ in); length (excluding radar) 14.54 m (47 ft 8½ in), (including SN-2 aerials) 16.5 m (54 ft 1½ in); height 4.85 m (15 ft 11 in); wing area 54.5 m^2 (586.63 sq ft)
Armament: aircraft illustrated, four 20-mm MG 151 cannon in ventral compartment each with 200 rounds

In the spring of 1944 RAF heavy bombers were being hacked down in droves. The cause was ascribed to concentrations of flak (AAA), and the bombers continued to cruise through the German sky like so many lighthouses, emitting up to three sets of radar signals, whilst so blind underneath that there was not so much as a porthole, let alone a gun. The fact that most of the losses were due to night-fighters emerged gradually, and it was near the end of the war before it was belatedly realised that many of these formated under the bomber and fired upwards in a perfect no-deflection shot. The most formidable night-fighter was almost unknown until, by a fantastic piece of luck, the crew of 4R+UR, a Ju 88G-1 of 7/NJG 2, became hopelessly lost on the night of 12/13 July 1944. They had been looking for minelaying Stirlings and had suffered compass failure. Eventually they homed on a radio beacon which seemed in the right direction, found an airfield and landed. They had brought the vital SN-2 radar and FuG 227 **Flensburg** ***to RAF Woodbridge, Suffolk. Unfortunately their aircraft did not have upward-firing guns but just four MG 151 cannon in the ventral box. The*** **Hirschgeweih** ***(stag's antlers) aerials of the SN-2 can be seen on the nose (a very few expert pilots had them on the rear fuselage). Wing dipole aerials received emissions from RAF Monica tail-warning radars and fed them to the*** **Flensburg** ***direction finder. The only things lacking were*** **schräge Musik** ***guns and*** **Naxos** ***for homing on*** H_2S.

Supermarine Spitfire F.Mk XIVE

***MV349** was a **S**pitfire **F.Mk XIVE** built by **S**upermarine and delivered in late 1944. As the markings show it immediately went out to the Far East Air Force, being shipped to **B**ombay and flown to **B**urma, where it operated with **RAF N**o. 28 **S**qn on the Malayan front until the end of the war. The actual end of fighting came just as **N**o. 28 **S**qn, with the other squadrons, was being readied to go aboard carriers from where they were to fly off to Malayan airfields during the final assault in that theatre. As can be seen, **MV349** was fitted with a low-level oblique camera aft of the cockpit, as in the **FR.Mk XIVE**, but did not have the latter's clipped wings. **S**tandard **E** armament was fitted: two 20-mm Hispano Mk II cannon and two 12.7-mm (0.5-in) **B**rowning machine-guns. The vertical tail had had to be increased in area to counter the longer nose, and the rear-view hood and cut-down rear fuselage ideally needed even greater fin area in compensation.*

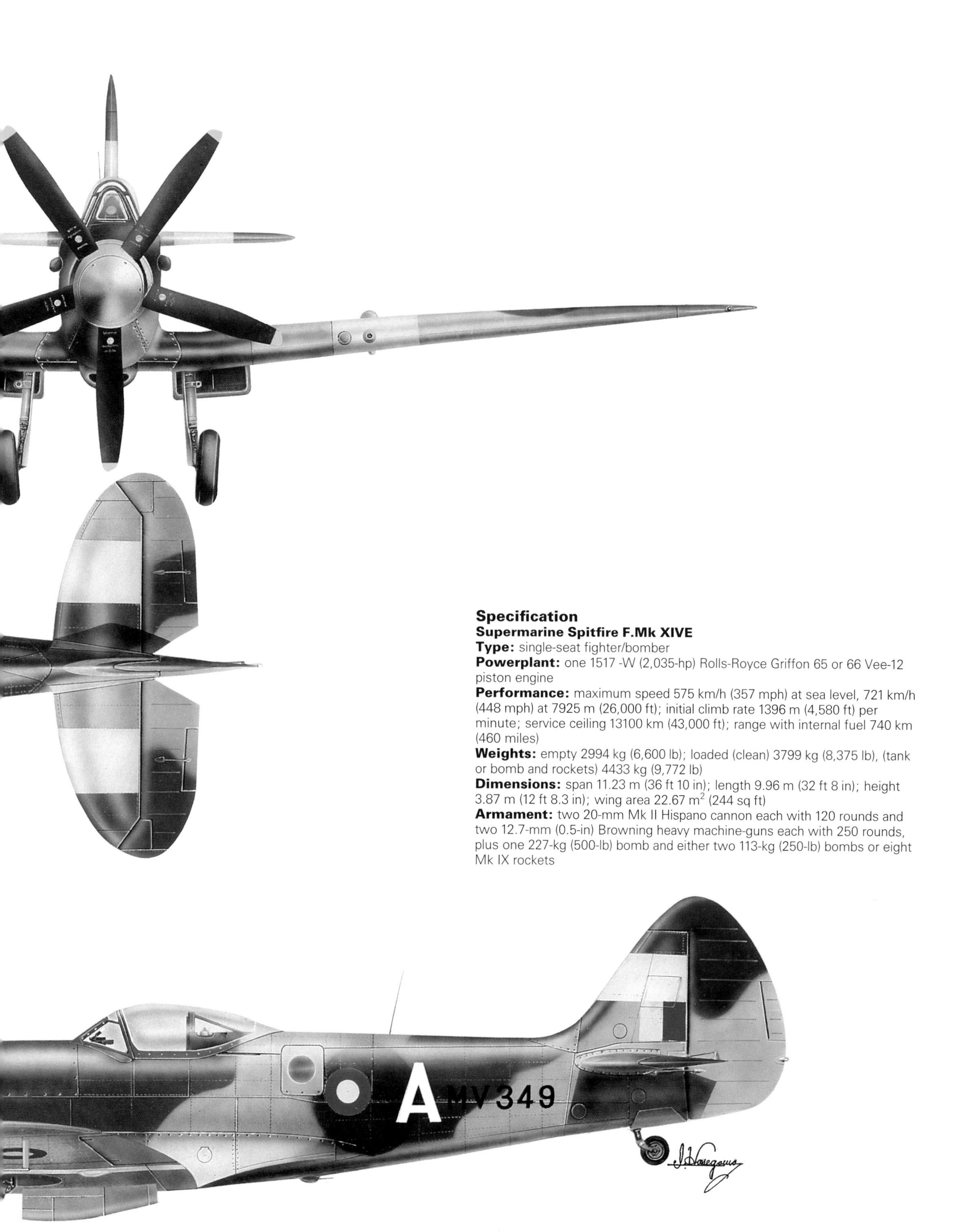

Specification

Supermarine Spitfire F.Mk XIVE

Type: single-seat fighter/bomber

Powerplant: one 1517 -W (2,035-hp) Rolls-Royce Griffon 65 or 66 Vee-12 piston engine

Performance: maximum speed 575 km/h (357 mph) at sea level, 721 km/h (448 mph) at 7925 m (26,000 ft); initial climb rate 1396 m (4,580 ft) per minute; service ceiling 13100 km (43,000 ft); range with internal fuel 740 km (460 miles)

Weights: empty 2994 kg (6,600 lb); loaded (clean) 3799 kg (8,375 lb), (tank or bomb and rockets) 4433 kg (9,772 lb)

Dimensions: span 11.23 m (36 ft 10 in); length 9.96 m (32 ft 8 in); height 3.87 m (12 ft 8.3 in); wing area 22.67 m^2 (244 sq ft)

Armament: two 20-mm Mk II Hispano cannon each with 120 rounds and two 12.7-mm (0.5-in) Browning heavy machine-guns each with 250 rounds, plus one 227-kg (500-lb) bomb and either two 113-kg (250-lb) bombs or eight Mk IX rockets

Petlyakov Pe-2FT

Specification
Petlyakov Pe-2FT

Type: three-seat tactical bomber
Powerplant: two 939-kW (1,260-hp) Klimov VK-105PF vee 12-cylinder piston engines
Performance: maximum speed 449 km/h (279 mph) at sea level and 580 km/h (360 mph) at 4000 m (13,125 ft); service ceiling 8800 m (28,870 ft); range with 1000-kg (2,205-lb) bombload 1315 km (817 miles)
Weights: empty 6200 kg (13,668 lb); maximum 8520 kg (18,783 lb)
Dimensions: span 17.11 m (56 ft 1⅔ in); length 12.78 m (41 ft 11 in); height 3.42 m (11 ft 2⅔ in); wing area 40.5 m^2 (436 sq ft)
Armament: provision for four FAB-100 (220.5-lb) bombs in internal bomb bay, two FAB-100 bombs in rear of engine nacelles and four FAB-250 (551-lb) bombs on external racks under centre section; two 7.62-mm (0.31-in) ShKAS machine-guns firing ahead aimed by pilot, MV-3 dorsal turret with single 12.7-mm (0.5-in) UBT, one ShKAS aimed by hand from rear ventral position (drawing shows UBS, very unusual) and one ShKAS aimed through left or right rear beam position

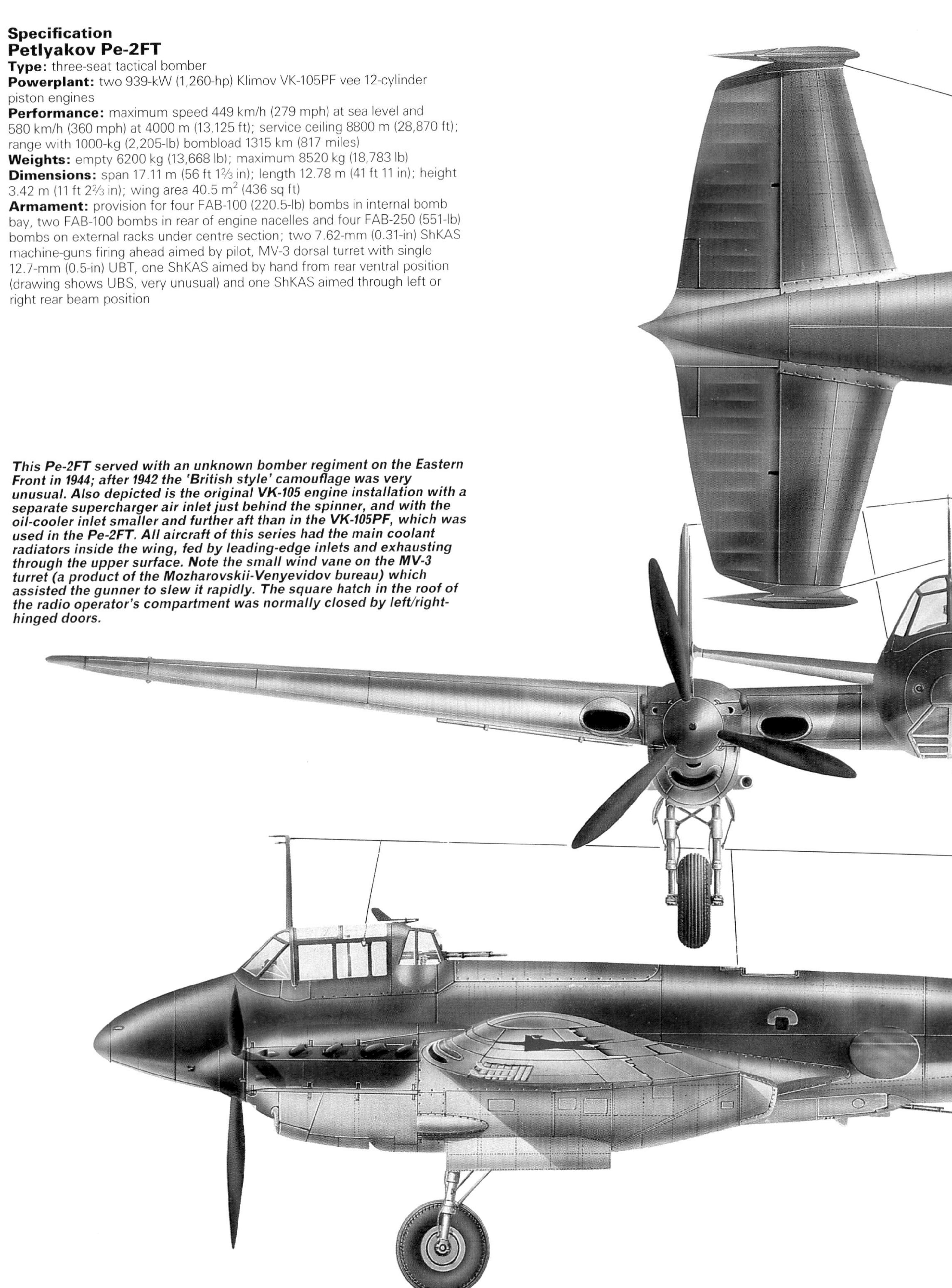

This Pe-2FT served with an unknown bomber regiment on the Eastern Front in 1944; after 1942 the 'British style' camouflage was very unusual. Also depicted is the original VK-105 engine installation with a separate supercharger air inlet just behind the spinner, and with the oil-cooler inlet smaller and further aft than in the VK-105PF, which was used in the Pe-2FT. All aircraft of this series had the main coolant radiators inside the wing, fed by leading-edge inlets and exhausting through the upper surface. Note the small wind vane on the MV-3 turret (a product of the Mozharovskii-Venyevidov bureau) which assisted the gunner to slew it rapidly. The square hatch in the roof of the radio operator's compartment was normally closed by left/right-hinged doors.

21

Yakovlev Yak-9

This Yak-9 was one of those equipping the Free French Normandie-Niémen regiment in 1944. It can be seen to be normal in all visible features, with armament of one ShVAK and one BS and with the blunt wingtips introduced early in production at the same time that the wing ribs were changed to aluminium. Many colour schemes were used by VVS front-line regiments, and in winter it was usual to add a rough coat of white on the upper surfaces.

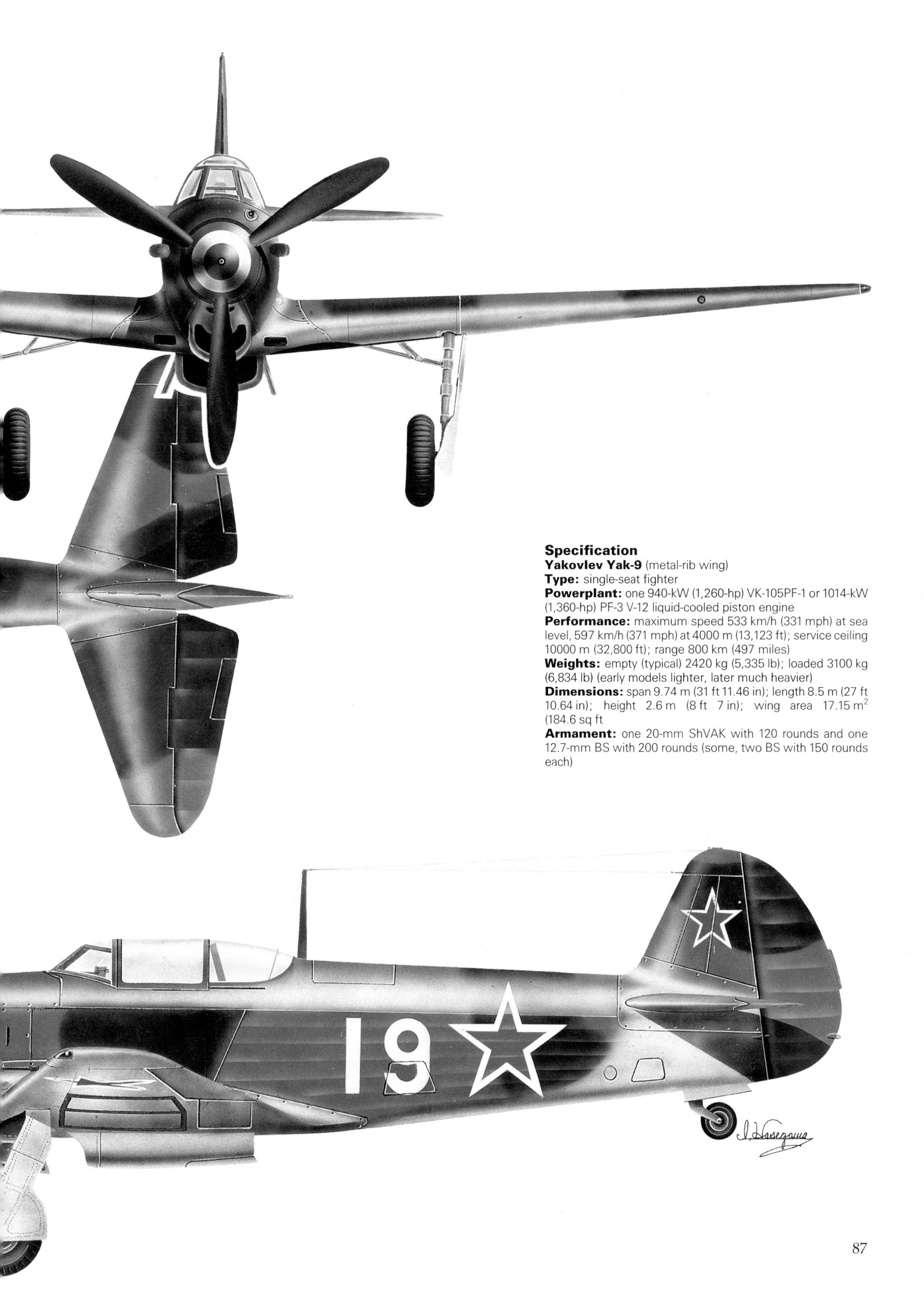

Specification
Yakovlev Yak-9 (metal-rib wing)
Type: single-seat fighter
Powerplant: one 940-kW (1,260-hp) VK-105PF-1 or 1014-kW (1,360-hp) PF-3 V-12 liquid-cooled piston engine
Performance: maximum speed 533 km/h (331 mph) at sea level, 597 km/h (371 mph) at 4000 m (13,123 ft); service ceiling 10000 m (32,800 ft); range 800 km (497 miles)
Weights: empty (typical) 2420 kg (5,335 lb); loaded 3100 kg (6,834 lb) (early models lighter, later much heavier)
Dimensions: span 9.74 m (31 ft 11.46 in); length 8.5 m (27 ft 10.64 in); height 2.6 m (8 ft 7 in); wing area 17.15 m^2 (184.6 sq ft
Armament: one 20-mm ShVAK with 120 rounds and one 12.7-mm BS with 200 rounds (some, two BS with 150 rounds each)

Martin B-26B-10-MA (Marauder Mk II)

The black and yellow diagonal stripes on the tail of this B-26C-45 (42-107812) identify it as belonging to the 387th Bombardment Group of the 98th Bombardment Wing, while the KS code indicates an aircraft of the 557th Squadron. For much of its time spent at Chipping Ongar in England between 25 June and 18 July 1944 the group was commanded by Colonel Jack E. Caldwell, and was heavily committed to daylight attacks on the V-weapon sites and airfields in Northern Europe. The aircraft as pictured here carries the invasion stripes applied at the time of the Normandy landings of June 1944; the squadron moved to Maupertius in France on 22 August 1944.

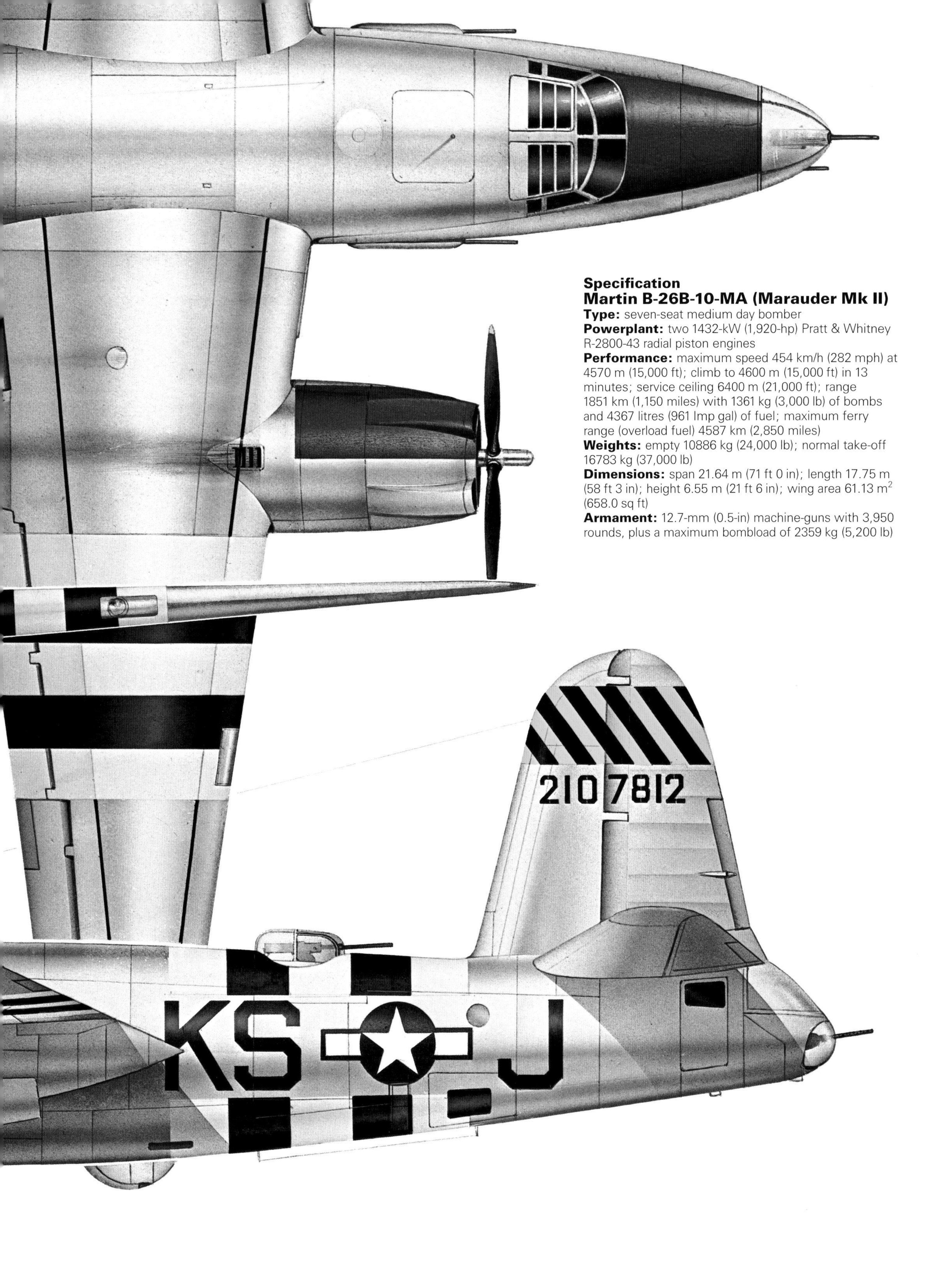

Specification
Martin B-26B-10-MA (Marauder Mk II)
Type: seven-seat medium day bomber
Powerplant: two 1432-kW (1,920-hp) Pratt & Whitney R-2800-43 radial piston engines
Performance: maximum speed 454 km/h (282 mph) at 4570 m (15,000 ft); climb to 4600 m (15,000 ft) in 13 minutes; service ceiling 6400 m (21,000 ft); range 1851 km (1,150 miles) with 1361 kg (3,000 lb) of bombs and 4367 litres (961 Imp gal) of fuel; maximum ferry range (overload fuel) 4587 km (2,850 miles)
Weights: empty 10886 kg (24,000 lb); normal take-off 16783 kg (37,000 lb)
Dimensions: span 21.64 m (71 ft 0 in); length 17.75 m (58 ft 3 in); height 6.55 m (21 ft 6 in); wing area 61.13 m^2 (658.0 sq ft)
Armament: 12.7-mm (0.5-in) machine-guns with 3,950 rounds, plus a maximum bombload of 2359 kg (5,200 lb)

North American P-51D Mustang

Though it was in service only in the final 18 months of World War II, the P-51D and basically identical K (different propeller) have since hogged almost all the Mustang limelight and also accounted for most of the 15,586 of all models produced. This aircraft, USAAF 1944-13926, served with the 361st Fighter Group of the 8th Air Force, at Bottisham (England) and in late 1944 at St Dizier (France).

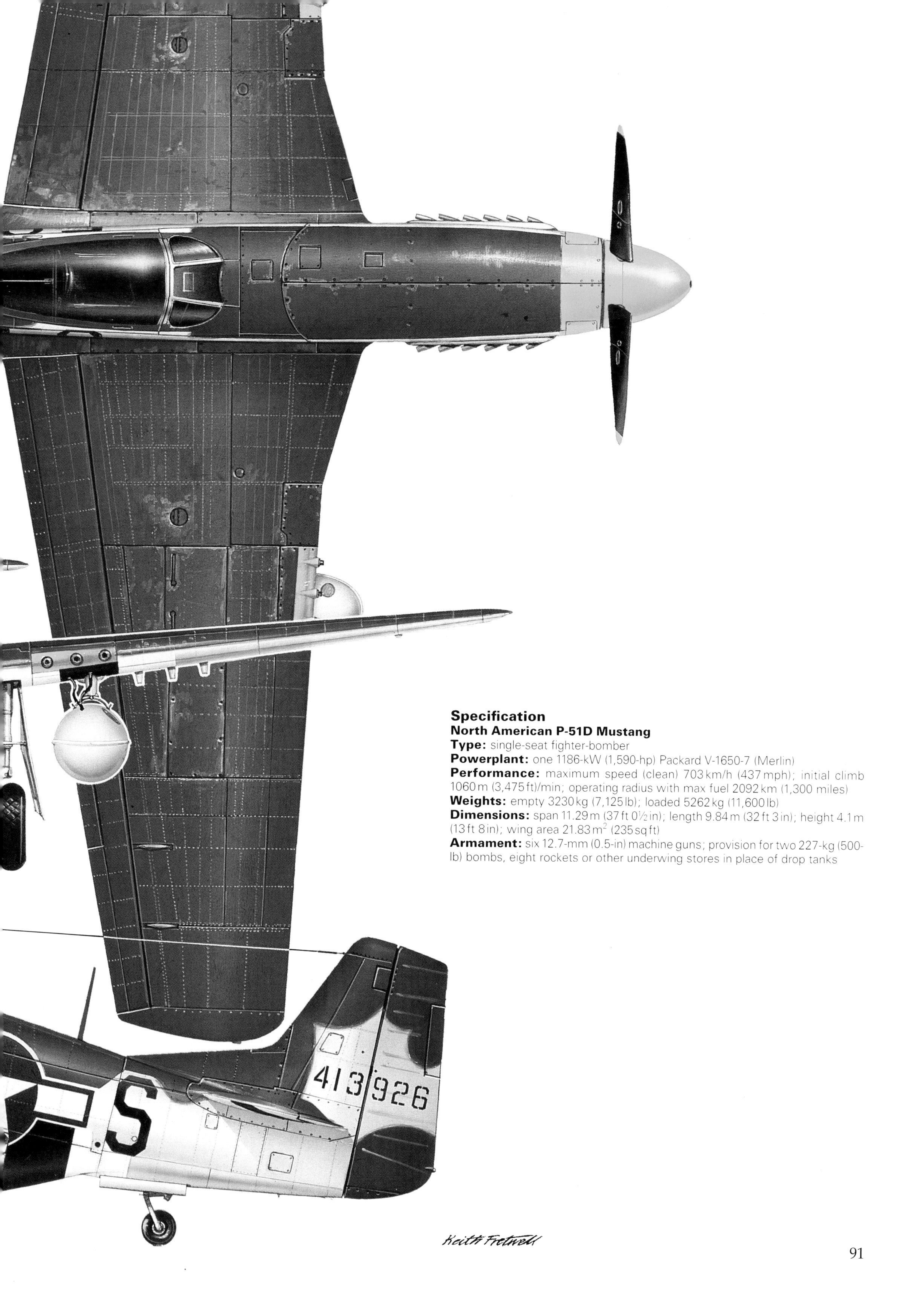

Specification
North American P-51D Mustang
Type: single-seat fighter-bomber
Powerplant: one 1186-kW (1,590-hp) Packard V-1650-7 (Merlin)
Performance: maximum speed (clean) 703 km/h (437 mph); initial climb 1060 m (3,475 ft)/min; operating radius with max fuel 2092 km (1,300 miles)
Weights: empty 3230 kg (7,125 lb); loaded 5262 kg (11,600 lb)
Dimensions: span 11.29 m (37 ft 0½ in); length 9.84 m (32 ft 3 in); height 4.1 m (13 ft 8 in); wing area 21.83 m^2 (235 sq ft)
Armament: six 12.7-mm (0.5-in) machine guns; provision for two 227-kg (500-lb) bombs, eight rockets or other underwing stores in place of drop tanks

Lavochkin La-5FN

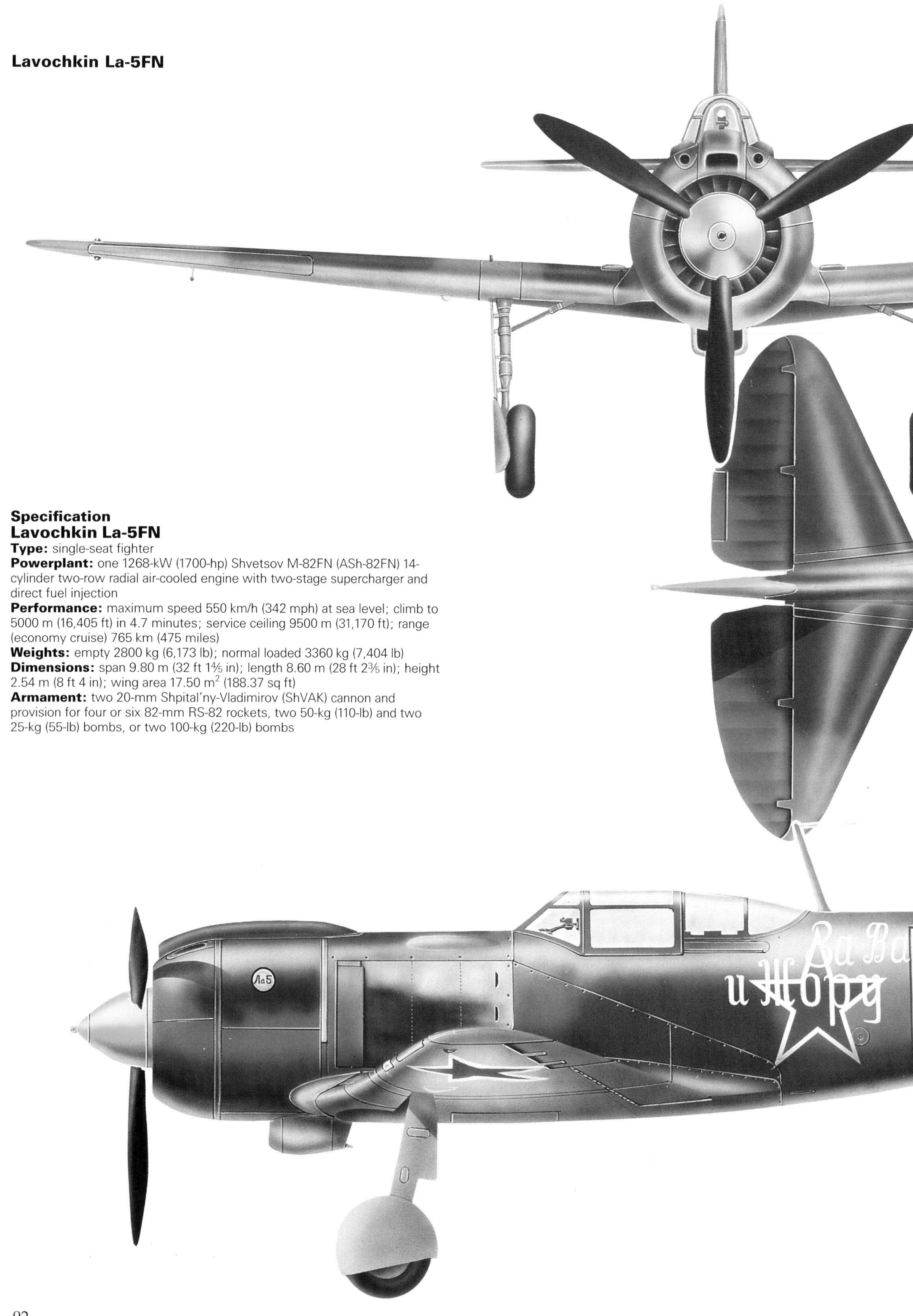

Specification
Lavochkin La-5FN

Type: single-seat fighter
Powerplant: one 1268-kW (1700-hp) Shvetsov M-82FN (ASh-82FN) 14-cylinder two-row radial air-cooled engine with two-stage supercharger and direct fuel injection
Performance: maximum speed 550 km/h (342 mph) at sea level; climb to 5000 m (16,405 ft) in 4.7 minutes; service ceiling 9500 m (31,170 ft); range (economy cruise) 765 km (475 miles)
Weights: empty 2800 kg (6,173 lb); normal loaded 3360 kg (7,404 lb)
Dimensions: span 9.80 m (32 ft 1⅘ in); length 8.60 m (28 ft 2⅗ in); height 2.54 m (8 ft 4 in); wing area 17.50 m^2 (188.37 sq ft)
Armament: two 20-mm Shpital'ny-Vladimirov (ShVAK) cannon and provision for four or six 82-mm RS-82 rockets, two 50-kg (110-lb) and two 25-kg (55-lb) bombs, or two 100-kg (220-lb) bombs

Illustrating one of several camouflage schemes applied to the La-5 during World War II, this La-5FN was flown by Captain P. J. Linkholetov of the 159th Gv IAP from Leningrad during the summer of 1944. Fuselage slogans proclaiming victory over the Germans and loyalty to the state were common on Soviet fighters, as were the outsize fuselage numbers. Although officially translated as 'directly boosted', the FN designation was dubbed by pilots as meaning* Frontu Nado*, 'frontal need'.

Northrop P-61B-1-NO

Specification
Northrop P-61B-1-NO
Type: three-seat night-fighter
Powerplant: two 1491-kW (2,000-hp) Pratt & Whitney R-2800-65 Double Wasp 18-cylinder radials
Performance: maximum speed (1678-kW/2,250-hp war emergency power) 589 km/h (366 mph) at 6096 m (20,000 ft); initial climb (military power 1491-kW/2,000-hp) 637 m (2,090 ft) per minute; range (long-range cruise power) 2172 km (1,350 miles) at 368 km/h (229 mph)
Weights: empty 10637 kg (23,450 lb); maximum overload 16420 kg (36,200 lb)
Dimensions: span 20.11 m (66 ft 0¾ in); length 15.11 m (49 ft 7 in); height 4.47 m (14 ft 8 in); wing area 61.53 m^2 (662.36 sq ft)
Armament: four 20-mm (0.78-in) M2 cannon each with 200 rounds; dorsal barbette with four 12.7-mm (0.5-in) Colt-Browning machine-guns each with 560 rounds; four external pylons each rated at up to 726 kg (1,600 lb) and able to carry bombs or other stores of up to this weight

This superb illustration shows one of the most famous P-61s of the Pacific theatre. Built as P-61B-1-NO, no. 42-39403, it was almost unique in having the dorsal gun barbette fitted; it did not come back into production until the P-61B-15 block, the first 200 (except for this aircraft and 42-39419) being turretless like the later P-61As. Other features of the B-model include a slightly longer nose, Curtiss Electric propellers with broader and more efficient blades, and four external pylons (here occupied by tanks) instead of two.

Northrop P-61 variants

XP-61: two prototypes, with R-2800-10 engines (41-19509/10)
YP-61: service-test aircraft (13), with Dash-10 engines (41-18876-88)
P-61A: production aircraft (200), from 38th without dorsal turret (often restored later); from 46th with water-injection Dash-65 engine (42-5485/5634 and -39348/39397)
P-61B: production aircraft (450), with Dash-65 engines; most with turret and four pylons, various equipment fits (42-39398/39757 and 43-8231/8320)
P-61C: production aircraft, with Dash-73 engines and CH-5 turbochargers, wet emergency rating 2089 kW (2,800 hp), Curtiss Electric paddle-blade hollow steel propellers, 692 km/h (430 mph) at high altitude (476 cancelled at VJ-Day and only 41, 43-8321/8361, delivered)
XP-61D: P-61As 42-5559 and 42-5587 re-engined with Dash-77 turbocharged engines
XP-61E: P-61Bs 42-39549 and 42-39557 rebuilt with slim nacelle, four 12.7-mm (0.5-in) guns in nose in place of radar, pilot and navigator under bubble hood (then largest piece of moulded Plexiglas ever attempted), 4382 litres (1,158 US gal) of internal fuel; first became XF-15
XP-61F: P-61C 43-8338 to be modified as P-61E but never completed
P-61G: production weather-reconnaissance aircraft modified from P-61Bs in 1945 (various numbers)
XF-15 Reporter: first XP-61E rebuilt as unarmed reconnaissance aircraft with six cameras in modified nose
XF-15A: P-61C (43-8335) modified with same nacelle as F-15 (visually distinguished from F-15 by large turbocharger ducts under engines)
F-15A Reporter: production aircraft (originally 175, only 36 actually built), based on part-complete P-61C airframes (45-59300/35)
F2T-1N: surplus P-61As (12) used as night-fighter trainers by US Marine Corps (Bu. Nos 52750/61)

403

Nakajima Ki-84-1a

Specification
Nakajima Ki-84-Ia
Type: single-seat fighter and fighter-bomber
Powerplant: one 1484-kW (1,990-hp) Nakajima Ha-45-21 18-cylinder air-cooled radial piston engine
Performance: maximum speed 631 km/h (392 mph) at 6120 m (20,080 ft); climb to 5000 m (16,405 ft) in five minutes 54 seconds; service ceiling 10500 m (34,450 ft); normal range 1695 km (1,053 miles)
Weights: empty 2660 kg (5,864 lb); maximum take-off 3890 kg (8,576 lb)
Dimensions: span 11.24 m (36 ft 10 7/16 in); length 9.92 m (32 ft 6 9/16 in); height 3.385 m (11 ft 1 1/4 in); wing area 21 m^2 (226.05 sq ft)
Armament: two 12.7-mm (0.5-in) Type 1 (Ho-103) machine-guns in the upper fuselage decking and two wing-mounted 20-mm Ho-5 cannon, plus two 250-kg (551-lb) bombs

A unit which had previously flown Ki-43s and Ki-44s in the defence of Okinawa was the 74th Sentai. Illustrated is a Ki-84-Ia operated by the 74th from Naruhatsu, Japan, in the summer of 1945. The superimposition of the Hinomarus on a white panel indicated a Home Defence aircraft.

Consolidated PBY-5A (OA-10A)

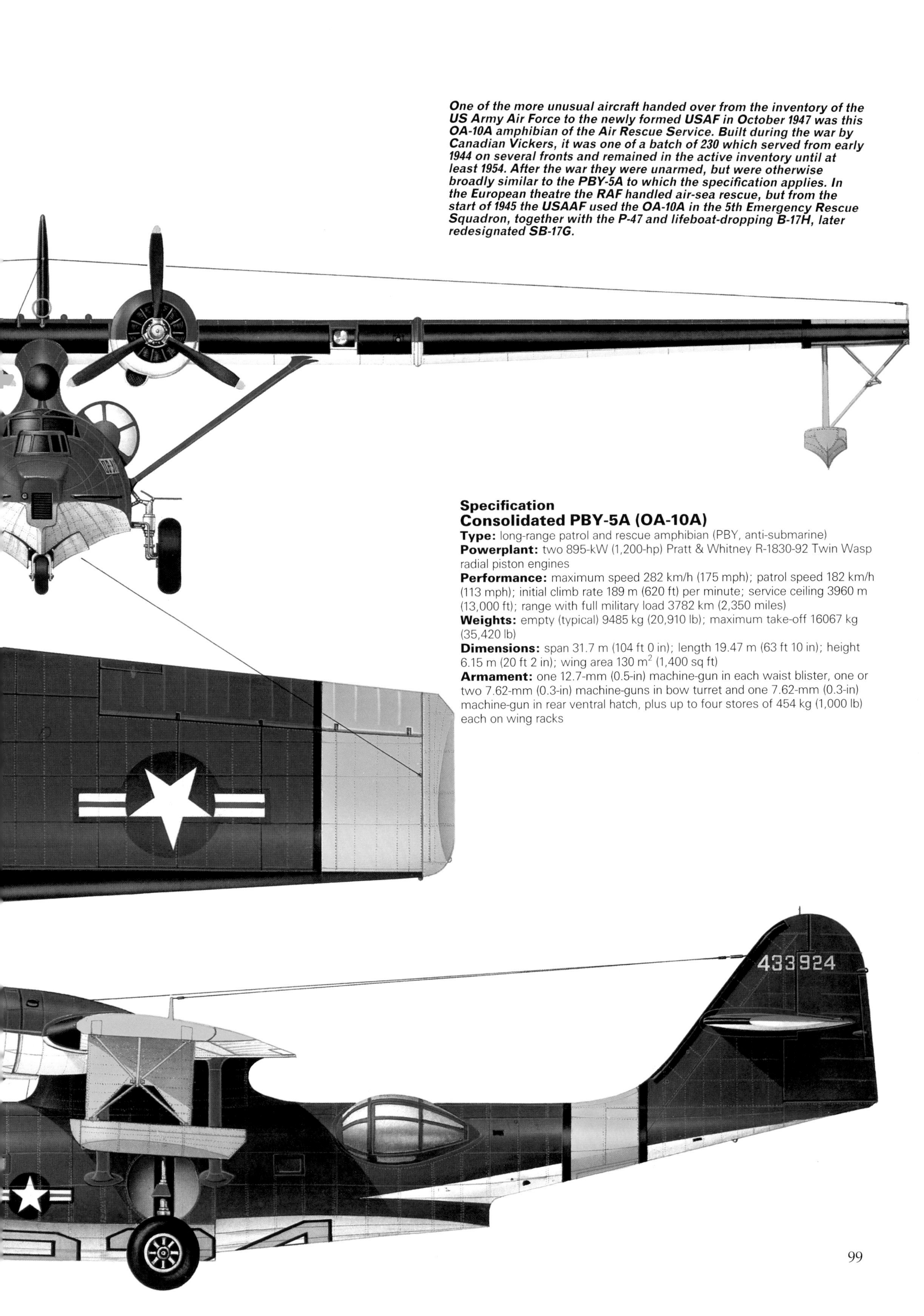

One of the more unusual aircraft handed over from the inventory of the US Army Air Force to the newly formed USAF in October 1947 was this OA-10A amphibian of the Air Rescue Service. Built during the war by Canadian Vickers, it was one of a batch of 230 which served from early 1944 on several fronts and remained in the active inventory until at least 1954. After the war they were unarmed, but were otherwise broadly similar to the PBY-5A to which the specification applies. In the European theatre the RAF handled air-sea rescue, but from the start of 1945 the USAAF used the OA-10A in the 5th Emergency Rescue Squadron, together with the P-47 and lifeboat-dropping B-17H, later redesignated SB-17G.

Specification
Consolidated PBY-5A (OA-10A)

Type: long-range patrol and rescue amphibian (PBY, anti-submarine)
Powerplant: two 895-kW (1,200-hp) Pratt & Whitney R-1830-92 Twin Wasp radial piston engines
Performance: maximum speed 282 km/h (175 mph); patrol speed 182 km/h (113 mph); initial climb rate 189 m (620 ft) per minute; service ceiling 3960 m (13,000 ft); range with full military load 3782 km (2,350 miles)
Weights: empty (typical) 9485 kg (20,910 lb); maximum take-off 16067 kg (35,420 lb)
Dimensions: span 31.7 m (104 ft 0 in); length 19.47 m (63 ft 10 in); height 6.15 m (20 ft 2 in); wing area 130 m^2 (1,400 sq ft)
Armament: one 12.7-mm (0.5-in) machine-gun in each waist blister, one or two 7.62-mm (0.3-in) machine-guns in bow turret and one 7.62-mm (0.3-in) machine-gun in rear ventral hatch, plus up to four stores of 454 kg (1,000 lb) each on wing racks

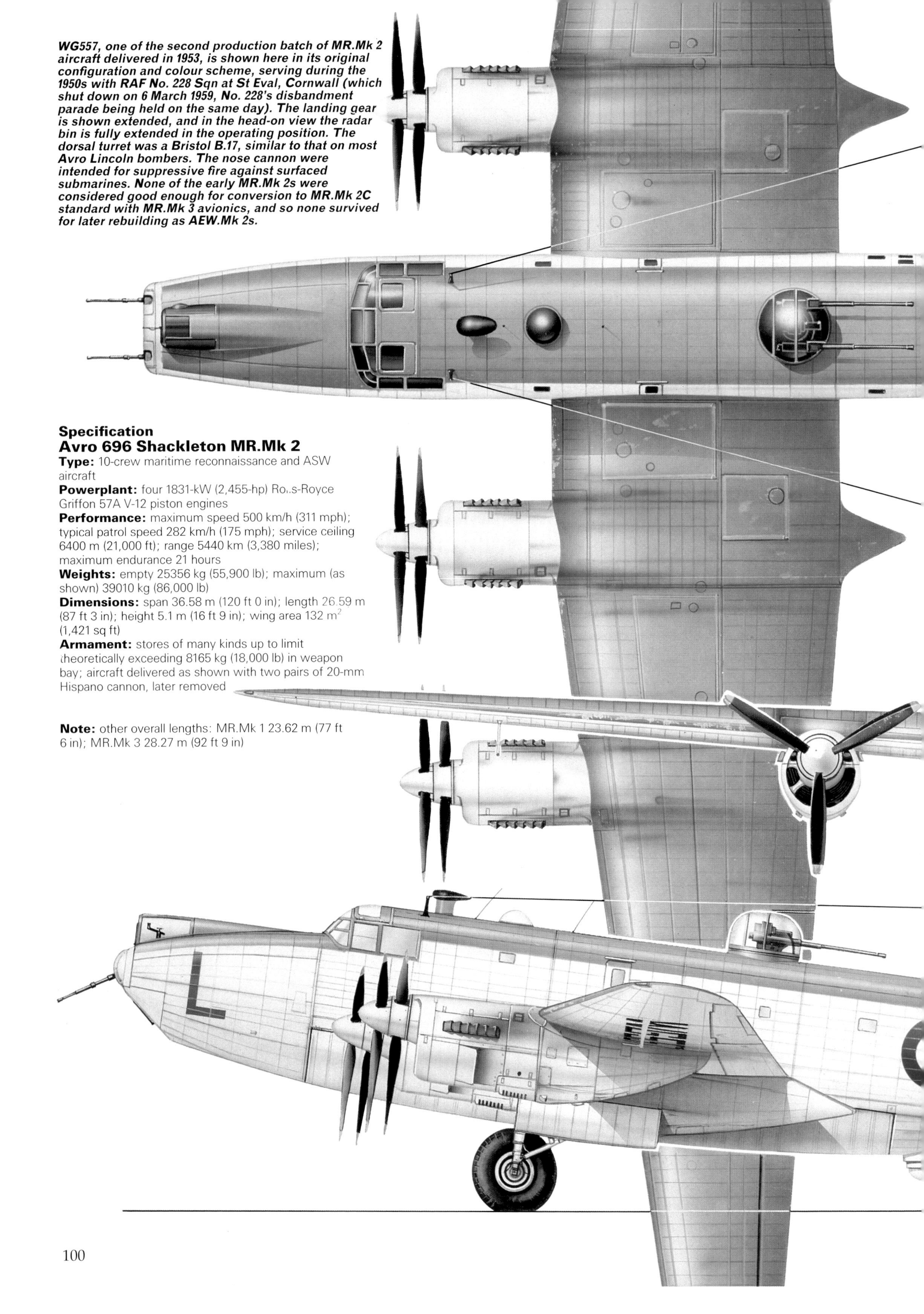

WG557, one of the second production batch of MR.Mk 2 aircraft delivered in 1953, is shown here in its original configuration and colour scheme, serving during the 1950s with RAF No. 228 Sqn at St Eval, Cornwall (which shut down on 6 March 1959, No. 228's disbandment parade being held on the same day). The landing gear is shown extended, and in the head-on view the radar bin is fully extended in the operating position. The dorsal turret was a Bristol B.17, similar to that on most Avro Lincoln bombers. The nose cannon were intended for suppressive fire against surfaced submarines. None of the early MR.Mk 2s were considered good enough for conversion to MR.Mk 2C standard with MR.Mk 3 avionics, and so none survived for later rebuilding as AEW.Mk 2s.

Specification
Avro 696 Shackleton MR.Mk 2

Type: 10-crew maritime reconnaissance and ASW aircraft
Powerplant: four 1831-kW (2,455-hp) Ro..s-Royce Griffon 57A V-12 piston engines
Performance: maximum speed 500 km/h (311 mph); typical patrol speed 282 km/h (175 mph); service ceiling 6400 m (21,000 ft); range 5440 km (3,380 miles); maximum endurance 21 hours
Weights: empty 25356 kg (55,900 lb); maximum (as shown) 39010 kg (86,000 lb)
Dimensions: span 36.58 m (120 ft 0 in); length 26.59 m (87 ft 3 in); height 5.1 m (16 ft 9 in); wing area 132 m^2 (1,421 sq ft)
Armament: stores of many kinds up to limit theoretically exceeding 8165 kg (18,000 lb) in weapon bay; aircraft delivered as shown with two pairs of 20-mm Hispano cannon, later removed

Note: other overall lengths: MR.Mk 1 23.62 m (77 ft 6 in); MR.Mk 3 28.27 m (92 ft 9 in)

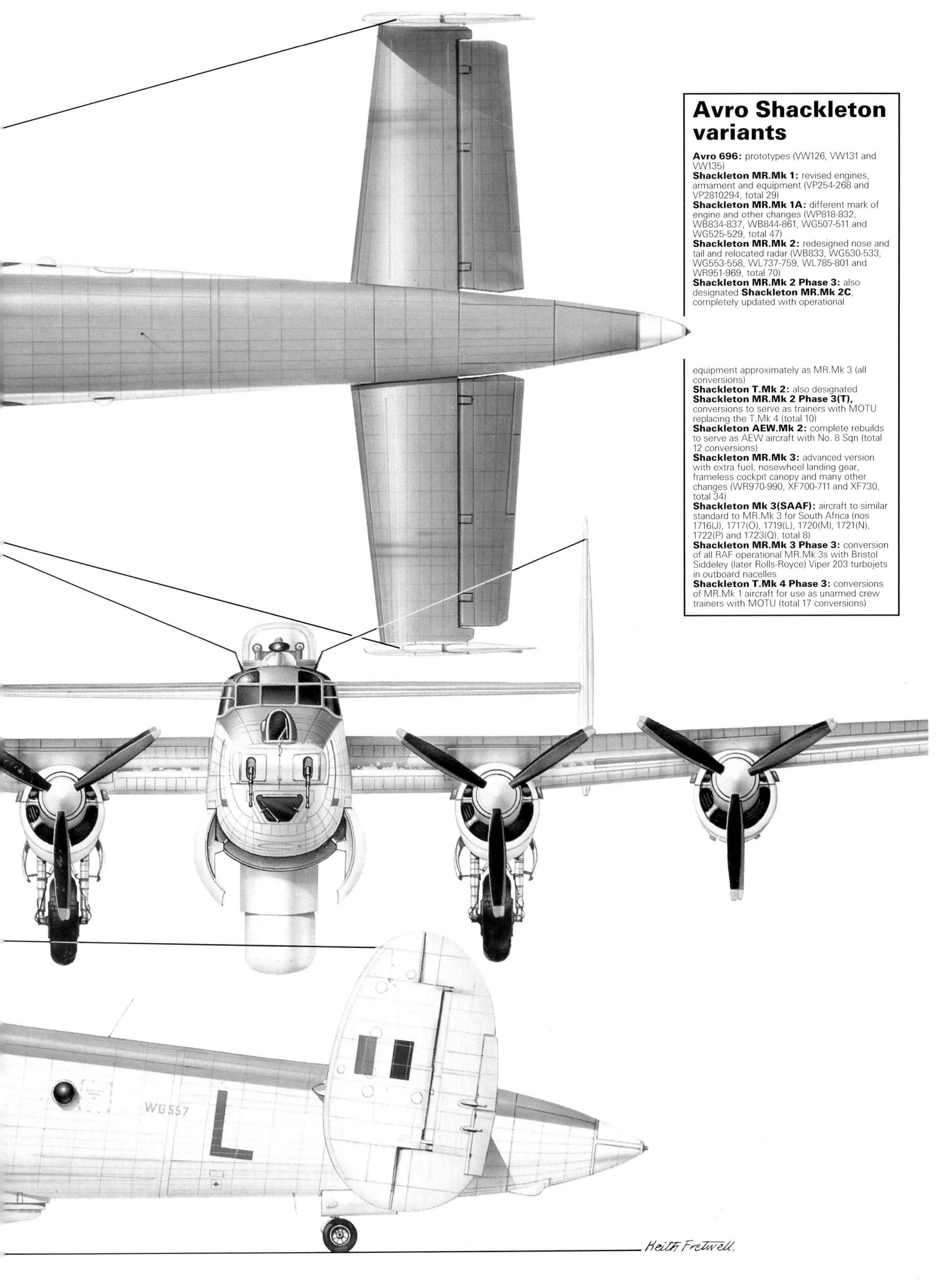

Avro Shackleton variants

Avro 696: prototypes (VW126, VW131 and VW135)
Shackleton MR.Mk 1: revised engines, armament and equipment (VP254-268 and VP2810294, total 29)
Shackleton MR.Mk 1A: different mark of engine and other changes (WP818-832, WB834-837, WB844-861, WG507-511 and WG525-529, total 47)
Shackleton MR.Mk 2: redesigned nose and tail and relocated radar (WB833, WG530-533, WG553-558, WL737-759, WL785-801 and WR951-969, total 70)
Shackleton MR.Mk 2 Phase 3: also designated **Shackleton MR.Mk 2C**, completely updated with operational equipment approximately as MR.Mk 3 (all conversions)
Shackleton T.Mk 2: also designated **Shackleton MR.Mk 2 Phase 3(T),** conversions to serve as trainers with MOTU replacing the T.Mk 4 (total 10)
Shackleton AEW.Mk 2: complete rebuilds to serve as AEW aircraft with No. 8 Sqn (total 12 conversions)
Shackleton MR.Mk 3: advanced version with extra fuel, nosewheel landing gear, frameless cockpit canopy and many other changes (WR970-990, XF700-711 and XF730, total 34)
Shackleton Mk 3(SAAF): aircraft to similar standard to MR.Mk 3 for South Africa (nos 1716(J), 1717(O), 1719(L), 1720(M), 1721(N), 1722(P) and 1723(Q), total 8)
Shackleton MR.Mk 3 Phase 3: conversion of all RAF operational MR.Mk 3s with Bristol Siddeley (later Rolls-Royce) Viper 203 turbojets in outboard nacelles
Shackleton T.Mk 4 Phase 3: conversions of MR.Mk 1 aircraft for use as unarmed crew trainers with MOTU (total 17 conversions)

Specification
Convair B-36J Peacemaker
Type: intercontinental strategic bomber
Powerplant: six 2685-kW (3,600-hp) Pratt & Whitney R-4360-53 radial piston engines and four 2449-kg (5,400-lb) thrust General Electric J47-19 turbojets

Performance: maximum speed 661 km/h (411 mph) at 11095 m (36,400 ft); cruising speed 629 km/h (391 mph); service ceiling 12160 m (39,900 ft); range 10945 km (6,800 miles) with a 4536-kg (10,000-lb) bomb load
Weights: empty 77581 kg (171,035 lb); maximum take-off 185976 kg (410,000 lb)
Dimensions: span 70.10 m (230 ft); length 49.40 m (162 ft 1 in); height 14.22 m (46 ft 8 in); wing area 443.32 m^2 (4,772 sq ft)
Armament: 16 20-mm cannon in nose, tail and six fuselage turrets, plus a bomb load of up to 20866 kg (46,000 lb) depending on distance flown; normal bomb load was 4536 kg (10,000 lb) over a range of 10945 km (6,800 miles)

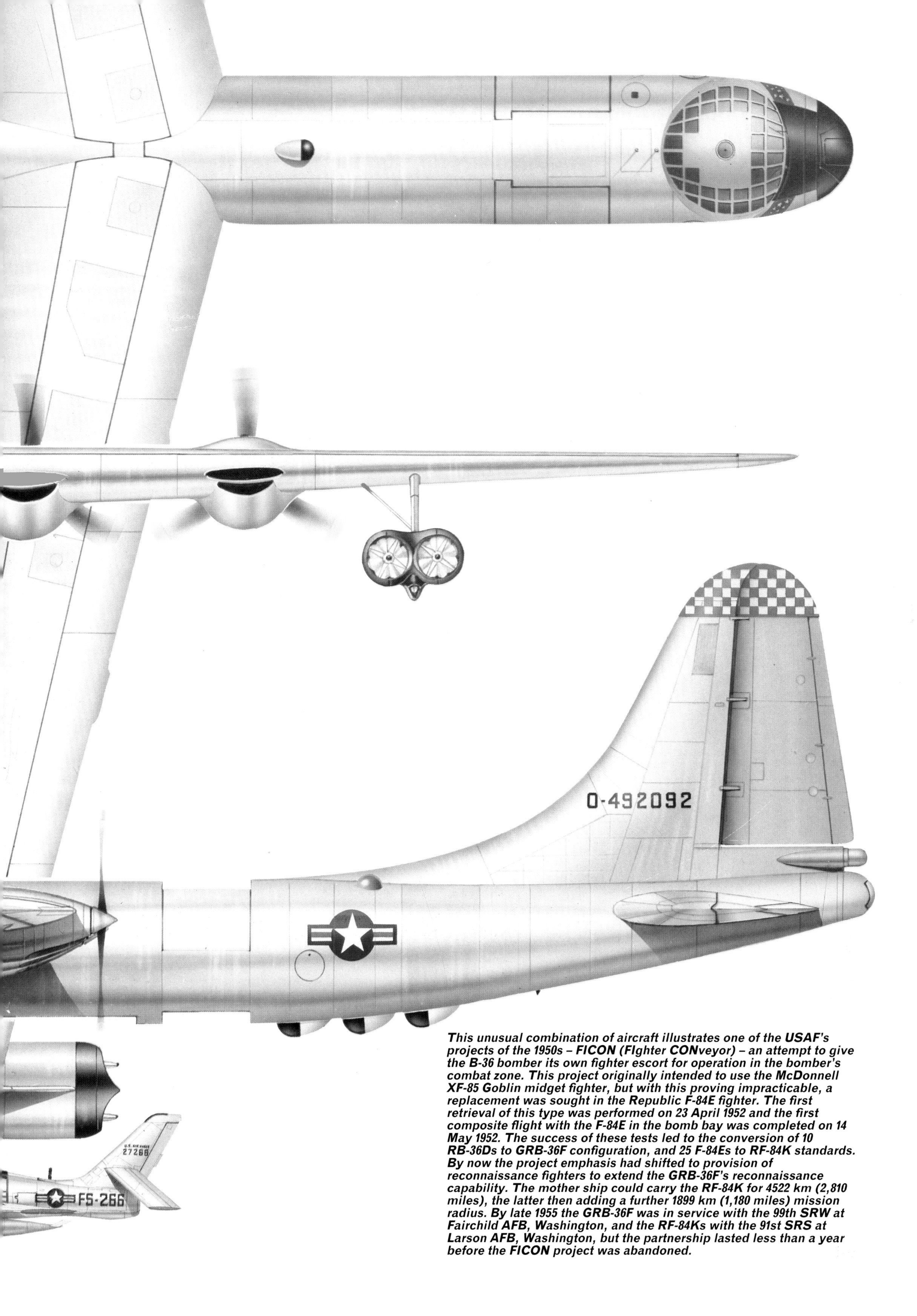

This unusual combination of aircraft illustrates one of the* USAF*'s projects of the 1950s –* FICON *(*FI*ghter* CON*veyor) – an attempt to give the* B-36 *bomber its own fighter escort for operation in the bomber's combat zone. This project originally intended to use the* McDonnell XF-85 Goblin *midget fighter, but with this proving impracticable, a replacement was sought in the* Republic F-84E *fighter. The first retrieval of this type was performed on 23 April 1952 and the first composite flight with the* F-84E *in the bomb bay was completed on 14 May 1952. The success of these tests led to the conversion of 10* RB-36Ds *to* GRB-36F *configuration, and 25* F-84Es *to* RF-84K *standards. By now the project emphasis had shifted to provision of reconnaissance fighters to extend the* GRB-36F*'s reconnaissance capability. The mother ship could carry the* RF-84K *for 4522 km (2,810 miles), the latter then adding a further 1899 km (1,180 miles) mission radius. By late 1955 the* GRB-36F *was in service with the 99th* SRW *at* Fairchild AFB, Washington*, and the* RF-84Ks *with the 91st* SRS *at* Larson AFB, Washington*, but the partnership lasted less than a year before the* FICON *project was abandoned.

Douglas A-1H Skyraider

Douglas Skyraider variants

XBT2D: first version with 1716-kW (2,300-hp) R-3350-24W; included prototypes of five other versions; total 25
AD-1: redesignation of **BT2D-1**, with 1865-kW (2,500-hp) R-3350-24W engine and strengthened structure; total 242
AD-1Q: ECM platform with jammer pod on left wing and ECM operator in fuselage cabin; total 35
AD-2: further strengthening, more fuel, 2014-kW (2,700-hp) R-3350-26W engine, mainwheel doors added; total 156
AD-2D: conversion to drone (RPV) directors
AD-2Q: ECM version; total 22
AD-2Q(U): further rebuild to tow Mk 22 target
AD-3: further strengthening, long-stroke main gears; Aeroproducts propeller and new canopy; total 124
AD-3E: conversion for ASW search
AD-3N: night attack version; total 15
AD-3Q: ECM version; total 23
AD-3S: anti-submarine attack, partner to AD-3E; all conversions
AD-3W: AEW version with improved APS-20 surveillance radar and two operators in fuselage cabin, plus auxiliary fins; total 31
AD-4: refined structure, cleared for great increase in gross weight from 8392 kg (18,500 lb) to 10886 kg (24,000 lb); P-1 autopilot, modified windscreen, improved radar (APS-19A) option; total 344
AD-4B: four cannon, provision for nuclear bombs; total 194
AD-4L: conversion for winter (Arctic)
AD-4N: night attack version with APS-19A; total 248
AD-4NA: night version stripped for day attack; total 23 plus conversions; redesignated **A-1D** from 1962
AD-4NL: winterised night version; total 36
AD-4Q: ECM version; total 39
AD-4W: AEW version as AD-3W; total 168
AD-5(A-1E): redesigned multi-role model with wide forward fuselage, side-by-side cockpit, longer fuselage, taller fin, side dive brakes removed (leaving ventral brake), four guns standard, provision for quick role conversions; cleared to 11340 kg (25,000 lb); total 212
AD-5N(A-1G): night attack version; total 239
AD-5Q(EA-1F): ECM conversions of 54 aircraft
AD-5S: (no 1962 designation) anti-submarine conversion
AD-5U(UA-1E): conversions as target tow/transport for 12 seats or 1361 kg (3,000 lb) of freight
AD-5W(EA-1E): AEW version; total 156
AD-6(A-1H): new standard close-support single-seater, LABS toss-bombing avionics and reinforced wing as AD-4B; total 713
AD-7(A-1J): further reinforced wing and main gear, 2275-kW (3,050-hp) R-3350-26WB engine; total 72

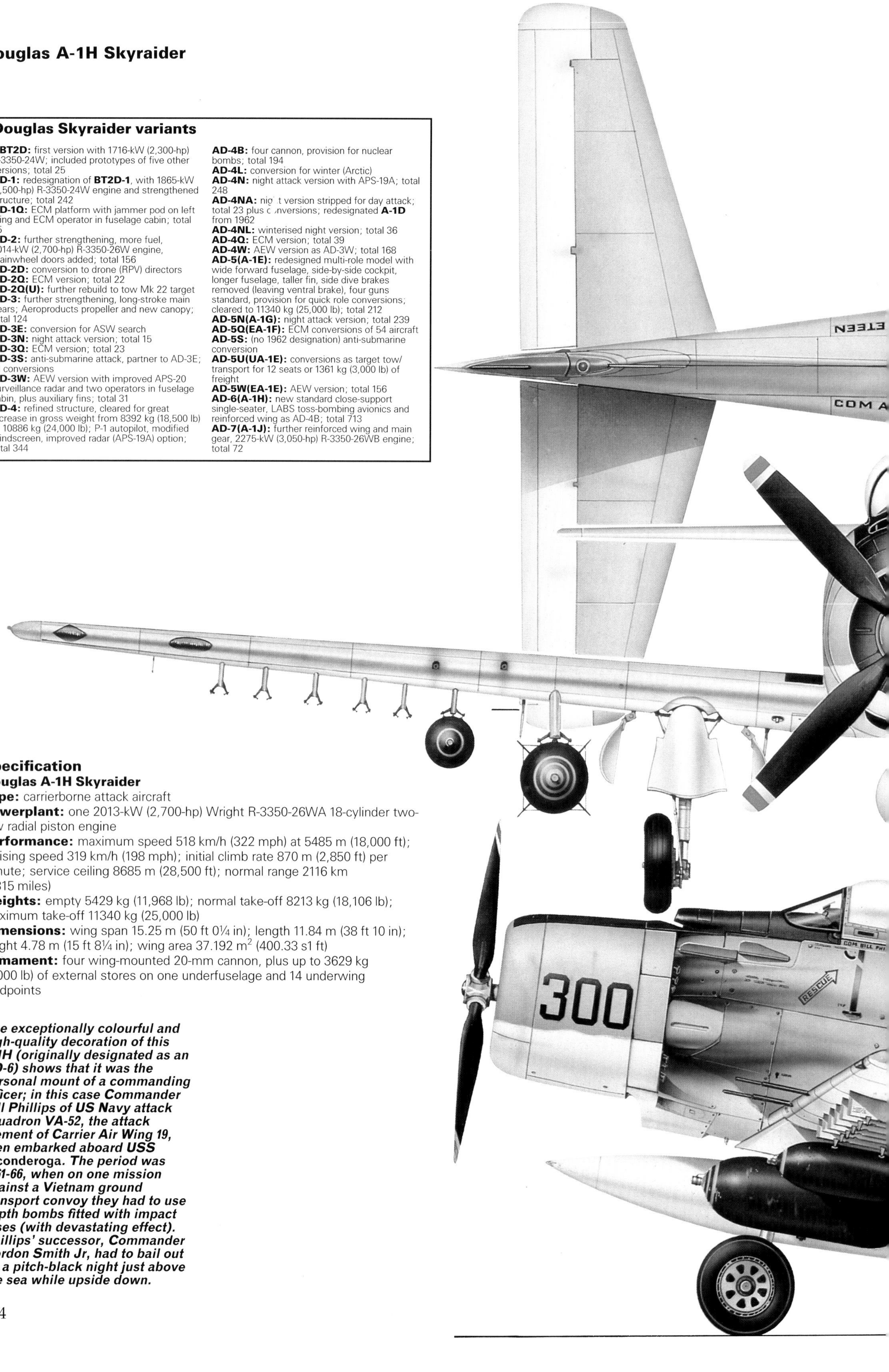

Specification
Douglas A-1H Skyraider
Type: carrierborne attack aircraft
Powerplant: one 2013-kW (2,700-hp) Wright R-3350-26WA 18-cylinder two-row radial piston engine
Performance: maximum speed 518 km/h (322 mph) at 5485 m (18,000 ft); cruising speed 319 km/h (198 mph); initial climb rate 870 m (2,850 ft) per minute; service ceiling 8685 m (28,500 ft); normal range 2116 km (1,315 miles)
Weights: empty 5429 kg (11,968 lb); normal take-off 8213 kg (18,106 lb); maximum take-off 11340 kg (25,000 lb)
Dimensions: wing span 15.25 m (50 ft 0¼ in); length 11.84 m (38 ft 10 in); height 4.78 m (15 ft 8¼ in); wing area 37.192 m^2 (400.33 s1 ft)
Armament: four wing-mounted 20-mm cannon, plus up to 3629 kg (8,000 lb) of external stores on one underfuselage and 14 underwing hardpoints

The exceptionally colourful and high-quality decoration of this A-1H (originally designated as an AD-6) shows that it was the personal mount of a commanding officer; in this case Commander Bill Phillips of US Navy attack squadron VA-52, the attack element of Carrier Air Wing 19, then embarked aboard USS **Ticonderoga**. ***The period was 1961-66, when on one mission against a Vietnam ground transport convoy they had to use depth bombs fitted with impact fuses (with devastating effect). Phillips' successor, Commander Gordon Smith Jr, had to bail out on a pitch-black night just above the sea while upside down.***

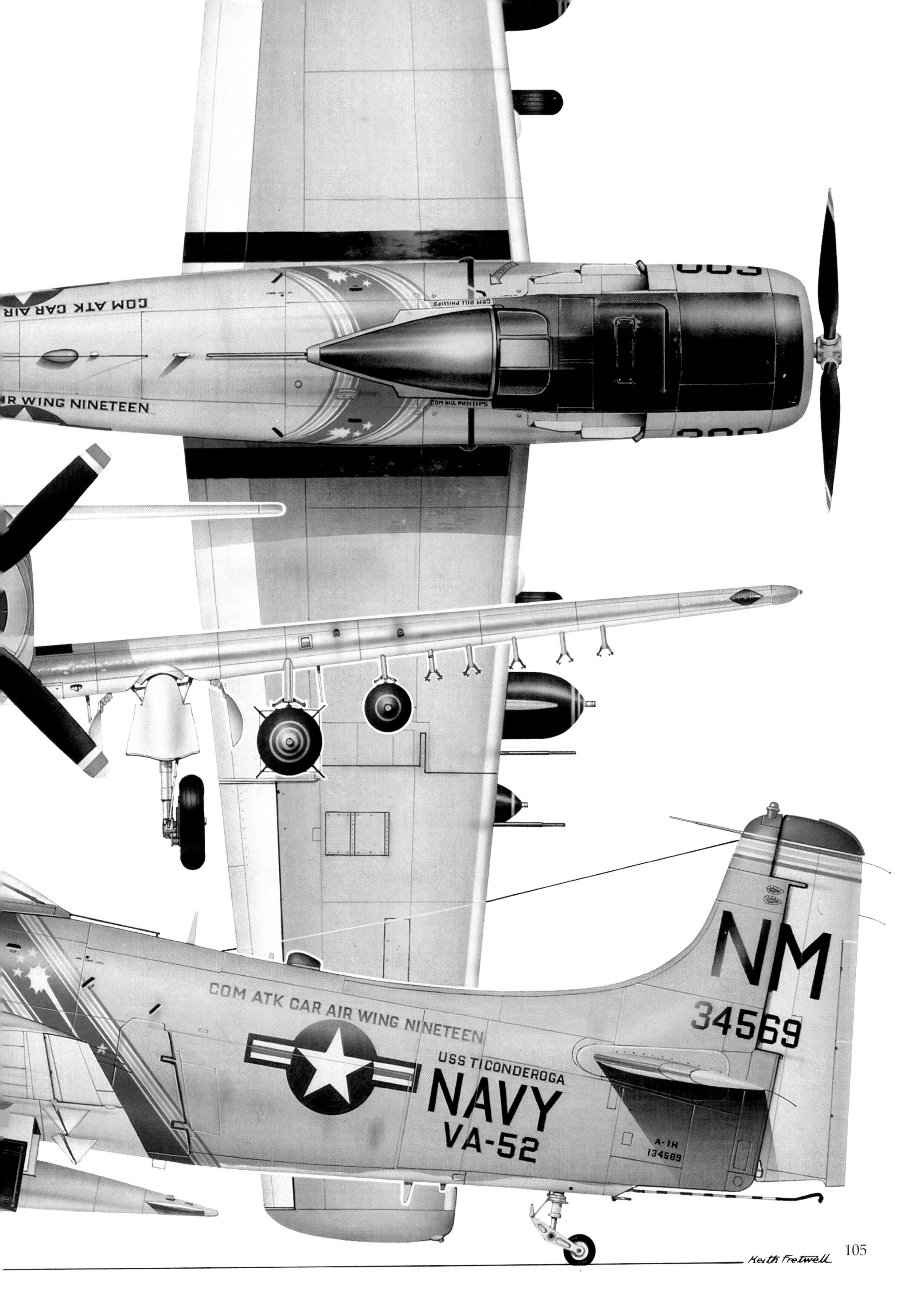
COM ATK CAR AIR
R WING NINETEEN
COM ATK CAR AIR WING NINETEEN
NM
34569
USS TICONDEROGA
NAVY
VA-52
A-1H
134569
Keith Fretwell

Lockheed Hercules AC-130A

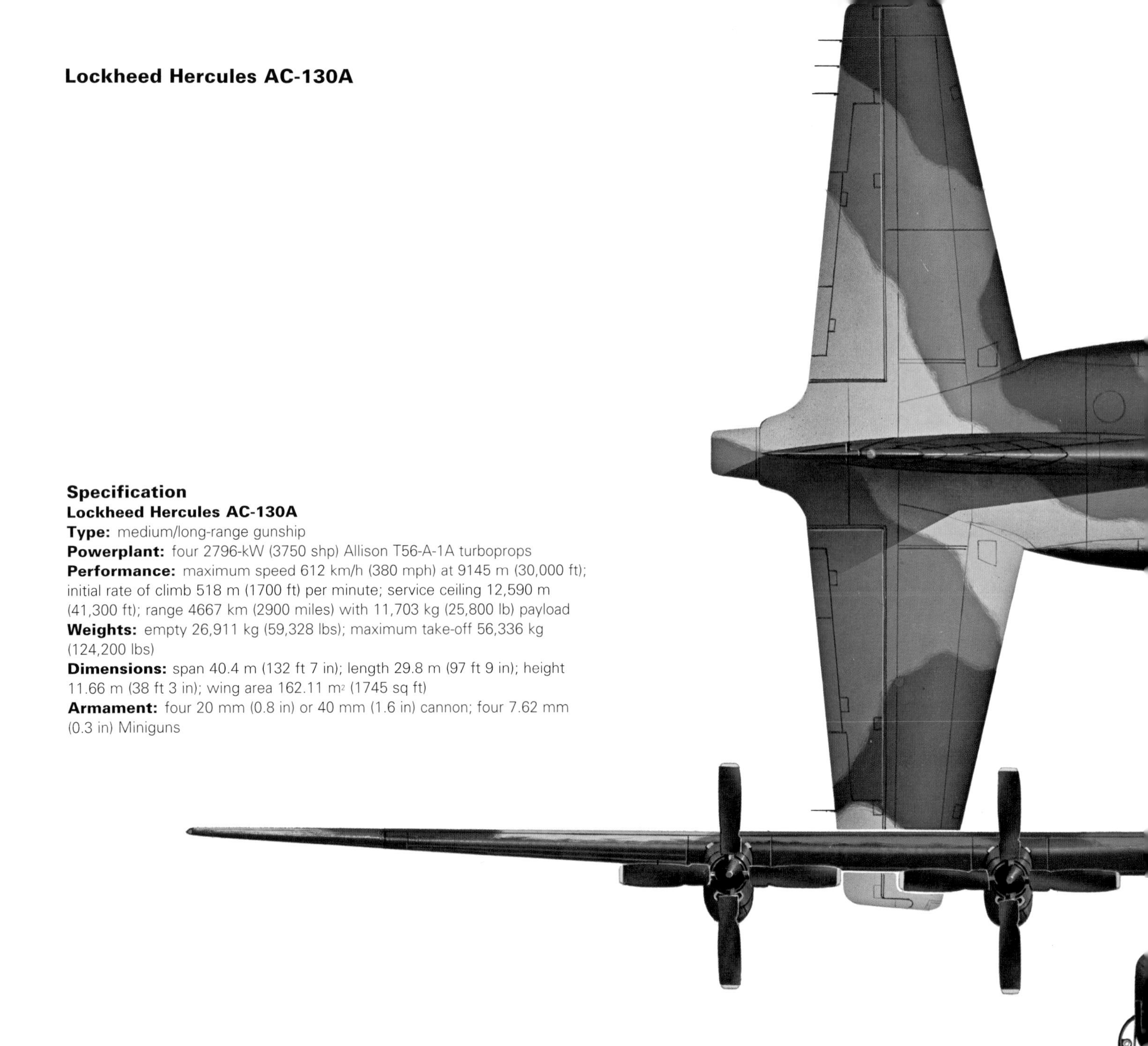

Specification

Lockheed Hercules AC-130A
Type: medium/long-range gunship
Powerplant: four 2796-kW (3750 shp) Allison T56-A-1A turboprops
Performance: maximum speed 612 km/h (380 mph) at 9145 m (30,000 ft); initial rate of climb 518 m (1700 ft) per minute; service ceiling 12,590 m (41,300 ft); range 4667 km (2900 miles) with 11,703 kg (25,800 lb) payload
Weights: empty 26,911 kg (59,328 lbs); maximum take-off 56,336 kg (124,200 lbs)
Dimensions: span 40.4 m (132 ft 7 in); length 29.8 m (97 ft 9 in); height 11.66 m (38 ft 3 in); wing area 162.11 m² (1745 sq ft)
Armament: four 20 mm (0.8 in) or 40 mm (1.6 in) cannon; four 7.62 mm (0.3 in) Miniguns

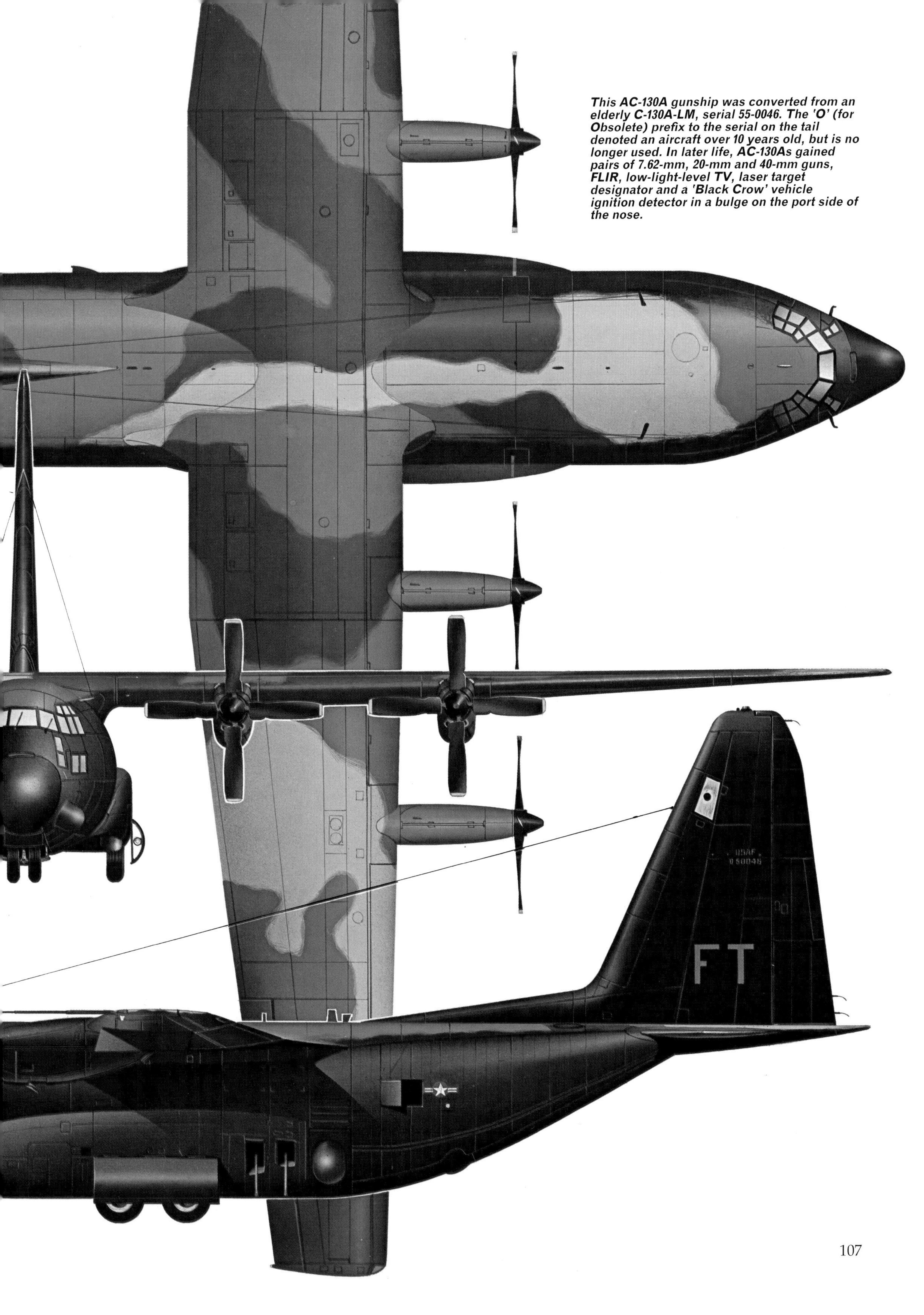

This AC-130A gunship was converted from an elderly C-130A-LM, serial 55-0046. The 'O' (for Obsolete) prefix to the serial on the tail denoted an aircraft over 10 years old, but is no longer used. In later life, AC-130As gained pairs of 7.62-mm, 20-mm and 40-mm guns, FLIR, low-light-level TV, laser target designator and a 'Black Crow' vehicle ignition detector in a bulge on the port side of the nose.

Previous experience with the IA-35 Huanquero and IA-50 Guarani transports were invaluable to the design process of the Pucará especially with regard to the wing design. Most of the rear fuselage is empty apart from control rods leading to the tail surfaces, air bottles and radio/electronics racks. The centre section contains a large fuel tank and the machine guns and cannon. This aircraft is one of six supplied to the Fuerza Aérea Uruguaya for counter-insurgency work, and carries Argentine-made 110-kg bombs in triplets under the fuselage (six) and under the wings (three).

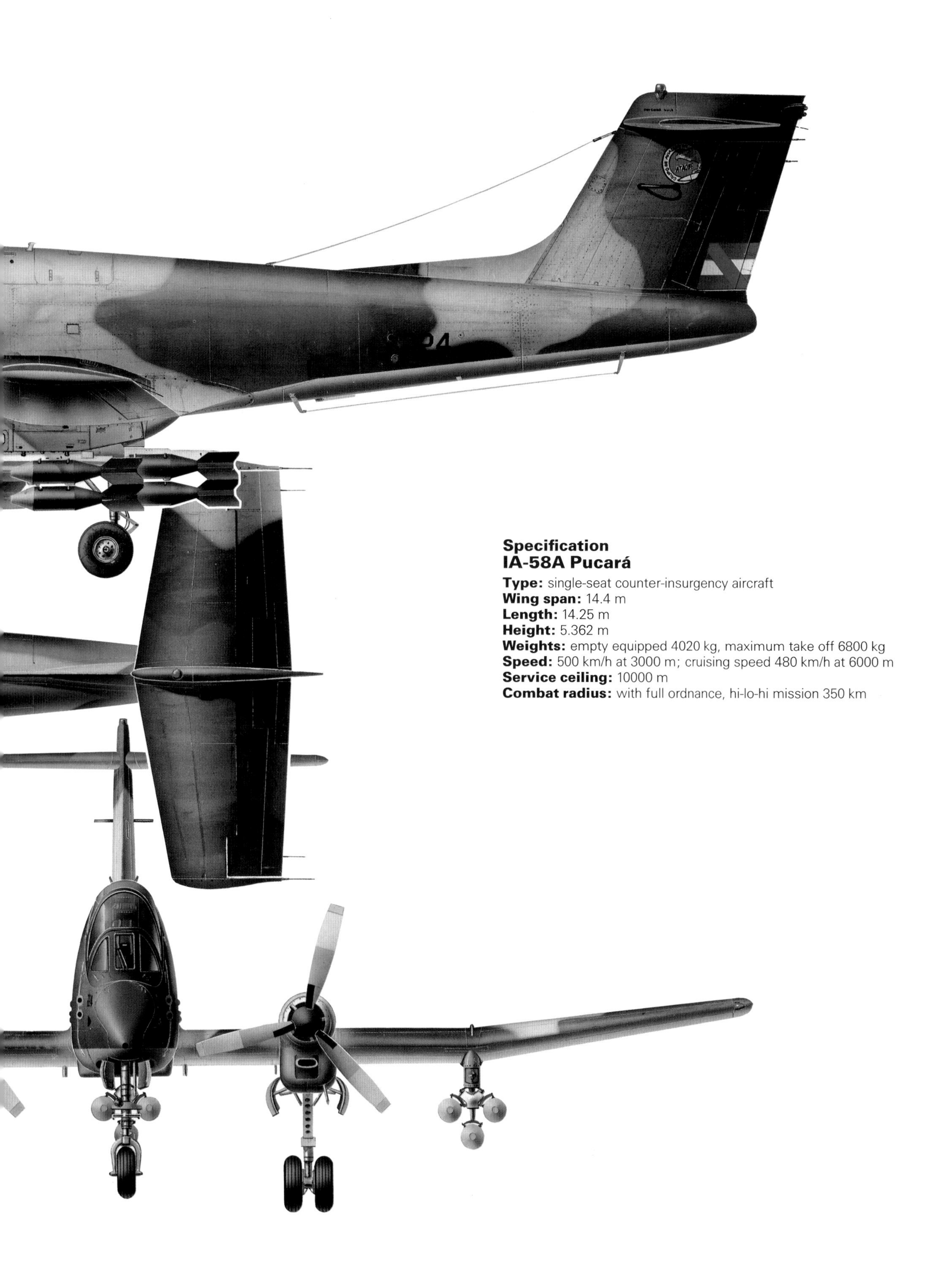

Specification
IA-58A Pucará
Type: single-seat counter-insurgency aircraft
Wing span: 14.4 m
Length: 14.25 m
Height: 5.362 m
Weights: empty equipped 4020 kg, maximum take off 6800 kg
Speed: 500 km/h at 3000 m; cruising speed 480 km/h at 6000 m
Service ceiling: 10000 m
Combat radius: with full ordnance, hi-lo-hi mission 350 km

Transall C-160

Specification

Transall C-160

Type: transport aircraft

Powerplant: two Rolls-Royce Tyne RTy.20 Mk 22 turboprops

Performance: maximum speed 513 km/h (319 mph) at 4875 m (16,000 ft); service ceiling 8230 m (27,000 ft); range 5095 km (3166 miles) with 8000 kg (17,637 lb) payload; initial rate of climb 396 m (1300 ft) per minute

Weights: empty 29,000 kg (63,934 lbs); maximum take-off 51,000 kg (112,436 lbs)

Dimensions: wingspan 40 m (131 ft 3 in); wing area 160 m^2 (1722 sq ft); length 32.4 m (106 ft 4 in); height 11.65 m (38 ft 3 in)

One of the Luftwaffe's three Transall units is LTG (Lufttransportgeschwader) 61 based at Landsberg. Like most German air force geschwader, or wings, it consists of at least two component squadrons. In this case, Nos 611 and 612 are those responsible for C-160 operations. The wing badge on the nose is a black goat on a mountain peak, while the less elaborate squadron badge is carried on the fin. Eighty-nine of Germany's 90 Transalls still survive, the original order having been reduced. All the aircraft have completed a Lebensdauer Verlängerungs Massnehmen (life extension programme) which involves the refitting of the navigation system and a reduction of the flight deck crew from four to three.